Contents

Grade 5 Standards—Reading: Informational Text

A. Key Ideas and Details	
	1. Quote accurately from a text when explaining what the text says explicitly and when drawing inferences from the text.
	2. Determine two or more main ideas of a text and explain how they are supported by key details; summarize the text.
	3. Explain the relationships or interactions between two or more individuals, events, ideas, or concepts in a historical, scientific, or technical text based on specific information in the text.
B. Craft and Structure	
	1. Determine the meaning of general academic and domain-specific words and phrases in a text relevant to a *grade 5 topic or subject area*.
	2. Compare and contrast the overall structure (e.g., chronology, comparison, cause/effect, problem/solution) of events, ideas, concepts, or information in two or more texts.
	3. Analyze multiple accounts of the same event or topic, noting important similarities and differences in the point of view they represent.
C. Integration of Knowledge and Ideas	
	1. Draw on information from multiple print or digital sources, demonstrating the ability to locate an answer to a question quickly or to solve a problem efficiently.
	2. Explain how an author uses reasons and evidence to support particular points in a text, identifying which reasons and evidence support which point(s).
	3. Integrate information from several texts on the same topic in order to write or speak about the subject knowledgeably.
D. Range of Reading and Level of Text Complexity	
	1. By the end of the year, read and comprehend informational texts, including history/social studies, science, and technical texts, at the high end of the grades 4–5 text complexity band independently and proficiently.

Visit www.creativeteaching.com to find out how this book correlates to Common Core and/or State Standards.

Reading Passages Specific Standards

Text	A.1	A.2	A.3	B.1	B.2	B.3	C.1	C.2	C.3	D.1
Earthquakes (p. 6)			✔	✔						✔
Hurricanes (p. 8)	✔	✔	✔					✔		✔
Tornado Alert! (p. 10)	✔	✔	✔							✔
Avalanches and Landslides (p. 13)	✔		✔	✔				✔		✔
Tsunami: Killer Waves (p. 15)	✔			✔						✔
Good Bones (p. 17)				✔				✔		✔
When a Bone Breaks (p. 19)	✔		✔	✔				✔		✔
Moving with Muscles (p. 21)	✔		✔							✔
Your Cardiovascular System (p. 23)	✔	✔	✔	✔						✔
Are You Getting Enough ZZZs? (p. 26)		✔	✔							✔
More Vitamin C, Please! (p. 28)			✔	✔						✔
Calories—We Need Them (p. 30)	✔	✔	✔							✔
Gluten and Lactose (p. 34)		✔	✔	✔						✔
Read That Label! (p. 36)		✔	✔	✔						✔
Mysteries of Stonehenge (p. 38)	✔		✔							✔
The Hoover Dam (p. 41)	✔		✔							✔
Famous Bridges (p. 44)			✔	✔						✔
Why Igloos Work (p. 46)		✔	✔	✔						✔
How Buildings Kill Birds (p. 48)		✔	✔							✔
How Does That Fly? (p. 50)			✔	✔						✔
Fill it Up! (p. 52)		✔	✔	✔						✔
Geothermal Electricity (p. 54)	✔	✔	✔	✔				✔		✔
Power From the Wind (p. 58)	✔				✔	✔			✔	✔
When Water Changes State (p. 62)		✔	✔	✔						✔
What Is a Landfill? (p. 64)	✔	✔	✔	✔				✔		✔
The Dinofish (p. 67)			✔							✔
Discovering King Tut's Tomb (p. 70)	✔			✔						✔
Discovering Exoplanets (p. 73)	✔		✔							✔
Who Rules Whom? (p. 76)	✔	✔	✔	✔						✔
What Does the President Do? (p. 78)	✔		✔	✔						✔
Harriet Tubman (p. 80)	✔	✔		✔						✔
Susan B. Anthony and Civil Rights (p. 82)	✔		✔	✔				✔		✔
Mark Twain (p. 84)	✔		✔					✔		✔
A Gift From Wali Dad (p. 86)	✔		✔							✔
The Wise Judge (p. 89)	✔		✔	✔						✔
King of the World (p. 92)			✔	✔						✔
The Teacher and the Thief (p. 95)	✔		✔							✔
A Great All-American Bird (p. 98)	✔	✔	✔	✔						✔

Introduction

Reading comprehension is the cornerstone of a child's academic success. By completing the activities in this book, children will develop and reinforce essential reading comprehension skills. Children will benefit from a wide variety of opportunities to practice engaging with text as active readers who can self-monitor their understanding of what they have read.

Children will focus on the following:

Identifying the Purpose of the Text
- The reader understands, and can tell you, why they read the text.

Understanding the Text
- What is the main idea of the text?
- What are the supporting details?
- Which parts are facts and which parts are opinions?

Analyzing the Text
- How does the reader's background knowledge enhance the text clues to help the reader answer questions about the text or draw conclusions?
- What inferences can be made by using information from the text with what the reader already knows?
- How does the information from the text help the reader make predictions?
- What is the cause and effect between events?

Making Connections
How does the topic or information they are reading remind the reader about what they already know?
- Text-to-self connections: How does this text relate to your own life?
- Text-to-text connections: Have I read something like this before? How is this text similar to something I have read before? How is this text different from something I have read before?
- Text-to-world connections: What does this text remind you of in the real world?

Using Text Features
- How do different text features help the reader?

Text Features

Text features help the reader to understand the text better. Here is a list of text features with a brief explanation on how they help the reader.

Contents	Here the reader will find the title of each section, what page each text starts on within sections, and where to find specific information.
Chapter Title	The chapter title gives the reader an idea of what the text will be about. The chapter title is often followed by subheadings within the text.
Title and Subheading	The title or topic is found at the top of the page. The subheading is right above a paragraph. There may be more than one subheading in a text.
Map	Maps help the reader understand where something is happening. It is a visual representation of a location.
Diagram and Illustration	Diagrams and illustrations give the reader additional visual information about the text.
Label	A label tells the reader the title of a map, diagram, or illustration. Labels also draw attention to specific elements within a visual.
Caption	Captions are words that are placed underneath the visuals. Captions give the reader more information about the map, diagram, or illustration.
Fact Box	A fact box tells the reader extra information about the topic.
Table	A table presents text information in columns and rows in a concise and often comparative way.
Bold and Italic text	**Bold** and *italic* text are used to emphasize a word or words, and signify that this is important vocabulary.

Earthquakes

Why Earthquakes Happen

Under the surface of Earth there are huge slabs of rock. These slabs are called **tectonic plates**. These plates move very **slowly**. Tectonic plates can **rub** against each other as they move in **different directions**.

Sometimes two tectonic plates get stuck as they rub against each other. **Force** builds up as the plates keep trying to move. Finally, there is enough force to make the plates move again. All the force that has built up makes the plates **move quickly** for a few moments. This movement causes the **surface of Earth** to **tremble** and **shake.** An earthquake is happening!

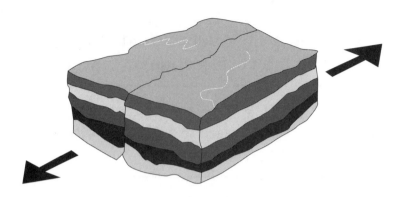

Force builds as two plates that are stuck keep trying to move.

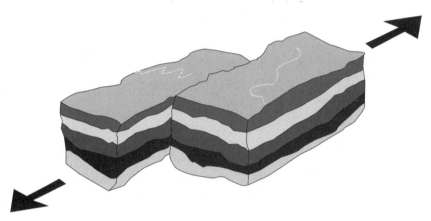

Finally, enough force builds up to make the plates move quickly.

Think about a time when you had trouble unscrewing the lid of a jar. The lid and the top of the jar were stuck together. You used your hand to put more and more force on the jar lid to make it move. Finally, there was enough force to make the lid move. This example gives you an idea of how force builds up to make tectonic plates move after they have been stuck together.

How Earthquakes Affect People

Some earthquakes are more **powerful** than others. In some places, earthquakes happen often, but the earthquakes are very weak. These earthquakes make the ground tremble just a tiny bit. People do not even notice that an earthquake has happened because they could not feel the ground moving. These earthquakes do not do any damage.

A powerful earthquake causes the ground to shake a lot. This shaking can do a lot of **damage** to **buildings** and other **structures**, such as bridges. In places where earthquakes tend to happen often, there are rules for building new structures strong enough to stand up to most earthquakes. Many older structures were built before the rules were put in place. Often, the worst damage from an earthquake happens to older buildings.

"Earthquakes"—Think About It

1. What are *tectonic plates*? Use specific details from the text to support your answer.

_____

_____

2. The overall structure of this text is cause and effect. Complete the chart to show causes and effects in the text. (Notice how one effect can cause something else to happen.)

Cause	Effect
Two tectonic plates get stuck as they rub against each other.	
	The plates move quickly for a few moments.
The plates move quickly for a few moments.	
An earthquake is so weak that people do not notice it.	
	There is a lot of damage to buildings and other structures.

3. What is one step people have taken to try to prevent structures from getting damaged during an earthquake?

_____

_____

4. Why are many older structures often damaged in an earthquake?

_____

_____

_____

_____

Hurricanes

What Is a Hurricane?

A hurricane is a huge storm that forms over **warm ocean water.** Hurricanes have winds that move in a circle. Hurricane winds are very **powerful**, and can move at speeds from 75 mph (120 kph) to over 186 mph (300 kph). Hurricanes can also bring large amounts of rain.

Hurricane winds rotate around a center called the **eye**. The eye is the **calmest** part of a hurricane. Winds in the eye are not very strong. Around the edge of the eye is an area called the **eye wall**. The eye wall has the **strongest** winds in a hurricane.

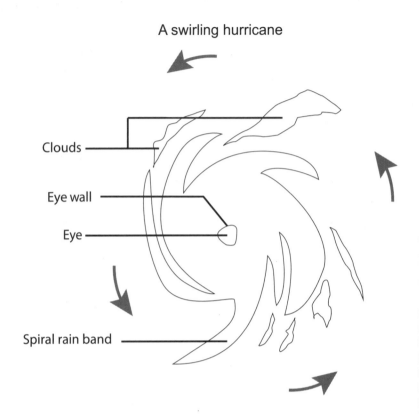

A swirling hurricane

Clouds

Eye wall

Eye

Spiral rain band

How Do Hurricanes Damage Structures?

Strong winds and heavy rain can do a lot of damage when a hurricane moves **over land**.

Wind: Hurricane winds can be strong enough to shatter windows. The winds can even knock over tall trees, which might fall on buildings or cars. Strong winds can pick up objects such as patio furniture and send them flying with **great force** into buildings, causing damage.

Strong winds can also cause a **storm surge** in areas along a **coast**. A storm surge happens when strong wind pushes water from the ocean onto land. When winds make a storm surge move quickly, the force of the moving water can be strong enough to move a house or destroy it. Storm surges cause **flooding** in areas near the coast.

Rain: Heavy rain from a hurricane can cause floods in areas that are not close to a coast. The floodwater can be very deep, sometimes reaching almost up to the roofs of houses. Water and mud seep into the houses and do a lot of damage. Wooden structures might not be safe after a flood. Water soaks into the wood and makes it weaker. There is danger that a wooden structure might collapse.

Fun Fact
- A hurricane name is retired, or taken off the list, if the storm has caused severe destruction or many deaths. A new name is then added to the list to replace it.

"Hurricanes"—Think About It

1. What is the overall structure of the text? Choose the correct answer and then give a reason to support your answer.

☐ Comparison (Showing how two or more things are similar and different)

☐ Question and answer (Asking questions and providing an answer to each question)

☐ Problem and solution (Identifying problems and explaining how to solve them)

_____

_____

_____

2. What are the two main ideas in the text?

First main idea: _____

_____

Second main idea: _____

_____

3. List two pieces of evidence the author gives to support the idea that hurricane winds are strong.

_____

_____

_____

4. A hurricane moves over a city. The strong winds suddenly die down. Then a short time later, the winds are strong again. What could explain this?

_____

_____

_____

5. Why might a house built of wood need to be torn down after a hurricane has caused deep floods?

_____

_____

_____

Tornado Alert!

A **tornado** is a **column** of air that is **spinning** very quickly. A tornado starts to form in a **storm cloud**. A spinning column of air starts to move down from the cloud. Before it touches the ground, the column of air is called a **funnel cloud**. When the funnel cloud touches the ground, it is called a tornado.

A funnel cloud stretches down from a storm cloud.

A funnel cloud that touches the ground is a tornado.

Tornadoes Are Powerful

A tornado can be one of the most **dangerous** storms in nature. Why? The wind in a **powerful** tornado is moving so quickly that it can destroy just about anything that gets in its way. In some tornadoes, the **wind speed** is over 186 mph (300 kph).

A powerful tornado can **tear apart** a house, send a car **flying** through the air, or **lift** a train car right off the train tracks. Less powerful tornadoes can still do a lot of damage. The wind can tear the roof off a house, snap large tree branches or even rip whole trees out of the ground. Falling trees and tree branches often damage homes and cars, and sometimes injure people.

10

Tornado Alert! (continued)

Tornadoes on the Move

A tornado does not stay in one place. Every tornado moves along with the cloud above it. Tornadoes move along the ground at different **speeds**. Some tornadoes move so slowly that they almost seem to stand still. A very fast tornado might move along the ground at about 62 mph (100 kph). An average tornado travels at about 31 mph (50 kph). Most tornadoes last for a few seconds to a few minutes, but some last for over one hour.

You can see where a tornado has traveled because it leaves a **path** of damaged or destroyed buildings, trees, and ripped-up ground behind it.

Weather reports will tell you if a **tornado watch** is in effect in your area. This means that the **weather conditions** are right for a tornado to form, but a tornado has not yet been seen. If you hear there is a **tornado warning** in your area, you need to get to a safe place. A tornado warning means that a tornado has been seen and might pass through your area.

Fun Facts

- Tornadoes are sometimes called "twisters."
- Tornadoes were measured on a five-level scale that measures their wind speed and how much damage they do. Up to February 2007, tornadoes were measured on the F Scale or Fujita Scale (say it like this: *Foo-jee-tuh*), named after the Japanese scientist who created the scale. Tornadoes are now measured on the EF Scale or Enhanced Fujita Scale, which has higher wind speeds than the old scale.
- The United States averages more than 1,000 tornadoes each year. Most of the tornadoes occur through an area nicknamed "Tornado Alley" that runs in a north-south direction, through the states in the center of the country.
- The longest-lived tornado ever was the Tri-State tornado of 1925. It affected the states of Missouri, Illinois, and Indiana. The tornado lasted for 3.5 hours and traveled along the ground for 219 miles (353 kilometers). The tornado caused a record 695 deaths, 2,027 injuries, and destroyed 15,000 homes.
- The largest tornado outbreak on record in the United States occurred on April 25–28, 2011. On those four days, over 350 tornadoes touched down across 15 states, causing at least 320 deaths, and more than 2,200 injuries.
- If you are caught outdoors or in a vehicle when a tornado is approaching, find a nearby ditch or a hollow in the ground, lie face down in it, and cover your head with your arms. Stay there until the tornado passes. Lying low like that, you are less likely to be picked up by a tornado and less likely to be hit by flying objects.

"Tornado Alert!"—Think About It

1. Could a tornado form on a windy day when the sky is clear? Tell why or why not.

_____

_____

_____

2. Use the diagrams to help you explain how a funnel cloud got its name.

_____

_____

_____

3. Tornado A left a longer path than Tornado B. Does this mean that Tornado A had to be traveling along the ground faster than Tornado B? Explain your answer.

_____

_____

_____

4. If a tornado is moving across the ground at 50 km/h, how fast is the cloud above it moving? Use information from the text to support your answer.

_____

_____

_____

5. Can weather experts tell when a tornado might form? Use information from the text to support your answer.

_____

_____

_____

6. Write two main ideas found in the last four paragraphs of the text.

_____

_____

Avalanches and Landslides

How are avalanches and landslides similar and different?

The Material That Falls
An **avalanche** is made of falling snow, ice, and rocks. A **landslide** is made of falling soil and rocks.

Where the Material Falls
Snow in an avalanche and soil in a landslide both fall down a **slope**. The slope is the side of a mountain or a tall hill.

What Makes the Material Fall
Imagine a **mountainside** covered with snow that does not move. The snow resists the pull of **gravity**, so it does not fall down the slope. A large snowfall can add a lot of snow on top of the snow that was already there. The snow on the mountainside is now so heavy that it cannot resist gravity, so gravity pulls the snow down the slope.

Landslides are also caused by **precipitation**. Rain or melting snow can lead to a landslide. The **particles** of soil on a dry slope rub against each other. Friction between the soil particles keeps the particles from moving. When the soil gets wet, there is water between the particles of soil. The water reduces the friction, so gravity can pull the soil down.

A landslide can damage structures such as houses.

A Trigger Event
Avalanches and landslides are usually started by a **trigger event**. The trigger event is something that makes the snow or soil **unstable**, so that gravity can start to pull it down the slope.

A trigger event is usually something that causes **vibrations**. The vibrations could come from an **earthquake**, an erupting **volcano**, or even a very **loud sound**. These vibrations make the snow or soil unstable, then gravity causes an avalanche or landslide.

"Avalanches and Landslides"—Think About It

1. What is the overall structure of this text? Choose the correct answer.

☐ Comparison (Showing how two or more things are similar and different)

☐ Problem/solution (Presenting one or problems and showing how to solve them)

☐ Chronology (Telling a series of events in the order that they happen)

2. The side of a mountain and a tall hill are examples of slopes. Explain what the word *slope* means.

_____

3. The text says that rain or melting snow can cause a landslide. What reason does the text give to explain this?

_____

_____

_____

4. Many houses have a sloped roof. Snow that builds up on a sloped roof can suddenly slide off. Use information from the text to explain why.

_____

_____

_____

5. Give two examples of ways that avalanches and landslides are similar.

_____

_____

6. Give two examples of ways that avalanches and landslides are different.

_____

_____

7. What is a *trigger event*? Give an example from the text.

_____

_____

Tsunami: Killer Waves

What Is a Tsunami?

A tsunami (say it like this: *soo-nah-mee*) is a series of huge **waves** of water. Most often, a tsunami is caused by an **earthquake** under the **ocean**. Some tsunamis are caused by erupting **volcanoes**. A tsunami can race across an ocean at up to 500 mph (805 kph). That is as fast as a jet **airplane** flies!

The 2011 Tsunami in Japan

On March 11, 2011, there was a major earthquake under the ocean close to Japan. The earthquake **damaged** buildings and left many people **injured** or **dead**. But the worst was still to come. About an hour after the earthquake, a tsunami hit Japan. In some areas, the tsunami waves were more than 131 ft. (40 m) high.

Damage to Structures

The damage caused by the tsunami was much greater than damage from the earthquake. One of the first places that the tsunami reached was a city called Sendai. The rushing water **swept away** cars, trucks, and even airplanes. Some buildings were **smashed** to pieces by the force of the water. Other buildings were **lifted** off their foundations. Videos showed entire buildings being **carried along** by the water.

A Human Tragedy

People estimate that more than 15,000 people were killed by the tsunami. Thousands of people were never found. More than 25,000 people were injured. Many people lost their homes, and others lost their jobs because the places where they worked had been destroyed.

Lending a Helping Hand

People everywhere were horrified by the effects of the tsunami. Governments, businesses, and citizens from around the world donated money to help the people of Japan after the tragedy. Many countries sent rescue teams to help find survivors.

"Tsunami: Killer Waves"—Think About It

1. What is a tsunami? Use specific details from the text to support your answer.

_____

_____

2. Minutes after the earthquake, Japan alerted people that there was danger of a tsunami. Why did the location of the earthquake make it more difficult for people in coastal areas to get to safety before the tsunami arrived?

_____

_____

_____

_____

3. When a tsunami wave picks up objects such as cars, trucks, and trees, the wave becomes even more dangerous to structures. Use information from the text and your ideas to explain.

_____

_____

_____

_____

4. After the tsunami warning, many people tried to escape danger areas in their cars. Why would it be difficult for a lot of people in cars to escape an area all at the same time? Include your own ideas.

_____

_____

_____

_____

5. How is the map helpful in this text?

_____

_____

Good Bones

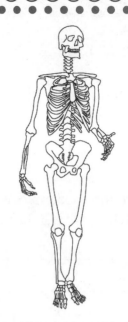

Your **skeleton** is your body's **framework**. This means it gives your body **shape**. It helps **support** different parts of your body. It helps **protect** what is inside your body, such as your lungs. Think about what your body would be like without a skeleton.

Your skeleton is made up of many different **bones**. These bones work together so you can **move** in many different ways. So it is important that your bones are **healthy**.

How Bones Change

Your bones are a living part of your body. When you were born, you had about 300 bones. Some baby bones are made from **cartilage**. Other baby bones are partly cartilage. Cartilage is softer than bone. That is why babies are so **flexible**. They can move their bones in ways that adults cannot. As a baby grows, the cartilage is replaced by bone, and some of the bones grow together. At around the age of 25, a person's bones stop growing. At that age, the adult skeleton has 206 hard bones.

Calcium and Bones

Calcium is a **mineral**. It is what helps bone grow to replace cartilage. It helps make bones strong. Calcium is very important when you are growing. Because bones grow for a long time, it is important for children and teenagers to get all the calcium they need. The most common source of calcium is **milk**. You can also get it from other **dairy products** such as cheese and yogurt. Calcium is also in dark green vegetables such as broccoli and kale. Some foods have calcium added to them. These are called **calcium-fortified** foods.

For calcium to work in your bones, it needs **vitamin D**. Your skin makes vitamin D when it is in sunlight. A small amount of vitamin D is found in fish such as salmon or tuna. Some foods, such as milk, are fortified with vitamin D.

Activity and Bones

Parts of your body, such as muscles, become stronger with exercise. Bones also get stronger with the right activity. The best activities to make bones stronger are called **weight-bearing** activities. These are activities in which you work against gravity, for example, walking, hiking, playing tennis, and lifting weights. Swimming and bicycling are good exercise, but not for your bones.

Many doctors think that the right exercise is just as important for making strong bones as calcium is. So make sure you get enough calcium and do the right activities for your bones. They have to last a lifetime.

"Good Bones"—Think About It

1. What do you think your body would look like without a skeleton? Why?

_____

_____

2. Give some examples of weight-bearing activities that are not in the text. Explain why the activities are weight-bearing.

_____

_____

_____

3. Explain why the number of bones in your body changes from 300 when you are a baby to 206 when you are an adult.

_____

_____

4. How is this text organized? How do the subheadings help you read the text?

_____

_____

_____

5. What do you think the word *flexible* means? Explain your thinking.

_____

_____

6. Why are babies so flexible? Use specific details from the text to support your answer.

_____

_____

7. The author says that bones are a living part of your body. What proof does the author give that they are alive?

_____

_____

When a Bone Breaks

Bones Are Strong

Bones can stand up to quite a bit of **force**. Think about the last time you tripped and **fell**. Your body hit the ground with a lot of force. You probably did not **break** a bone because your bones were **strong** enough to stand up to the force.

Did you know that bones can **bend**? Bones can bend a little when a strong force acts on them. If the bone bends too much, it will break. Think about breaking a pencil. When you first start to put force on a pencil, it will bend a little. If you **increase** the force you put on the pencil, it will break.

Setting Broken Bones

A doctor will take an **X-ray** to find out if a bone is broken. The X-ray also tells the doctor how to set a broken bone. The doctor has to move the pieces of the broken bone back to their normal position. **Setting** a broken bone is a way to make sure the bone **heals** properly.

Putting a Cast Around a Broken Bone

Once the broken bone has been set, it is important to keep the two broken pieces in the **proper position** until the bone is completely healed. Doctors often use a **cast** to make sure that the broken pieces of bone do not move while they heal.

A cast is a hard structure that goes on the outside of the body, over the broken bone. Some casts are made of bandages soaked in **plaster**. When the plaster dries, the cast is hard and stiff. Some casts are made of hard plastic.

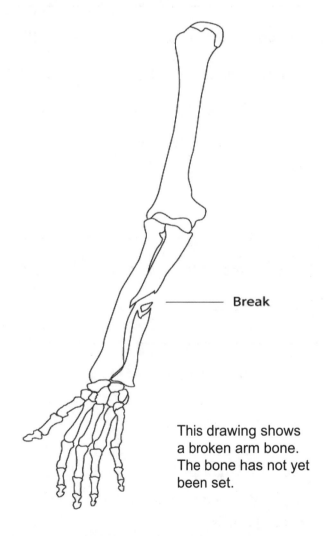

Break

This drawing shows a broken arm bone. The bone has not yet been set.

A Broken Bone Heals Itself

It can take from one to two months for a broken bone to heal. The bone makes many **new cells** to heal the break. These cells act like **glue**—they hold the broken pieces together and slowly make the bone as good as new.

"When a Bone Breaks"—Think About It

1. The author compares a bone with a pencil to help explain something about bones. What does the author want to explain?

_____

_____

2. What two reasons does the text give to explain why a doctor takes an X-ray?

_____

_____

3. What does "setting a bone" mean? Use specific details from the text to support your answer.

_____

_____

4. a) How long does a person with a broken bone need to wear a cast? Use information in the text to make an inference.

_____

_____

b) Write the sentence from the text that helped you make your inference.

_____

_____

5. Use information from the text to complete the chart of causes and effects.

Cause	Effect
	The pieces of broken bone are now back in their normal position.
A cast is put around the part of the body where the broken bone is.	
	The broken pieces of bone stick together and slowly make the bone as good as new.

Moving with Muscles

How Do Muscles Make You Move?

Muscles can do two things—they can **contract** and **relax**. A muscle gets shorter and thicker when it contracts. When the muscle relaxes, it gets longer and thinner.

Muscles make us move by working together in pairs. For example, the upper part of your arm has a **biceps** muscle and a **triceps** muscle (see the diagram below). This pair of muscles works together when you bend your arm at the elbow. As your arm bends, two things happen—the biceps muscle contracts and the triceps muscle relaxes. As you unbend your arm, the triceps muscle contracts and the biceps muscle relaxes.

How Do You Control Your Muscles?

When you want to move in a certain way, your **brain** sends **signals** to the muscles you need to use. When you want to bend your arm at the elbow, your brain sends out two signals. One signal goes to the biceps muscle and tells it to contract. Another signal goes to the triceps muscle and tells it to relax. Both muscles work together to make you bend your arm.

Can You Control All Your Muscles?

The muscles that you can control are called **voluntary** muscles. All the muscles that make your body move are voluntary muscles. You tell your body that you want to ride a bike or throw a ball. Your brain sends signals to the voluntary muscles that you need to use. You control your voluntary muscles.

Your body has muscles that you do not control. These are called **involuntary** muscles. These muscles work on their own. For example, your **heart** is an involuntary muscle. It contracts and relaxes as it beats. You do not need to think about making your heart beat—it beats on its own. That is why your heart keeps beating when you are asleep.

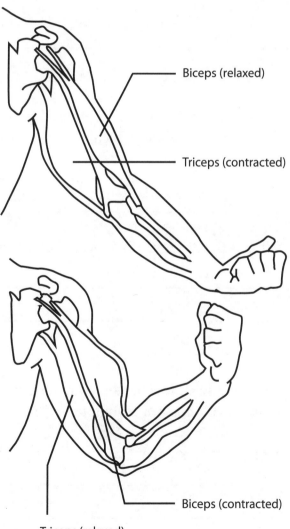

Biceps (relaxed)

Triceps (contracted)

Biceps (contracted)

Triceps (relaxed)

"Moving with Muscles"—Think About It

1. What is happening to a muscle when it contracts?

_____

_____

2. What is happening to a muscle when it relaxes?

_____

_____

3. Muscles work in pairs to make you move. If one muscle in a pair is contracting, what is the other muscle doing?

_____

_____

4. You decide that you want to jump. You do not use all of the muscles in your body to jump. How does your body know which muscles to use?

_____

_____

5. What is the difference between a voluntary and an involuntary muscle?

_____

_____

6. After you swallow a bite of food, muscles make the food move down to your stomach. Are these muscles voluntary or involuntary? Give a reason to support your answer.

_____

_____

_____

Your Cardiovascular System

A **system** is made up of **parts** that all work together to make something happen. Your **cardiovascular system** is made up of your **heart**, **blood**, and **blood vessels**. The cardiovascular system moves blood from your heart to every part of your body, then back to your heart again.

Heart

Your heart is a **muscle** about the size of your fist. When your heart beats, first it squeezes blood out of the heart and into blood vessels. Then it relaxes, which pulls more blood into the heart. When you are not being active, your heart beats about 70 times each minute. It beats faster when you are being active.

Blood

Most of your blood is a clear liquid called **plasma**. **Red blood cells** make blood look red. These blood cells carry **oxygen** to all the parts of your body. **White blood cells** help your body fight **germs**. **Platelets** are blood cells that work at **repairing** your body after an injury.

Blood Vessels

Blood vessels are **tubes** that your blood moves through. There are different types of blood vessels:

Arteries: These are blood vessels that carry blood away from the heart.

Veins: Veins are blood vessels that carry blood back to the heart.

Capillaries: Arteries and veins branch out into many smaller blood vessels, just like a large tree branch has many smaller branches on it. These smaller blood vessels are called capillaries.

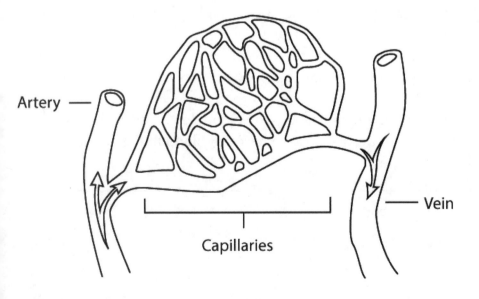

Capillaries in your body are much smaller than shown here. A human hair is about 10 times thicker than most capillaries.

Blood and Oxygen

One of the most important jobs of blood is to carry oxygen to all parts of your body. How does oxygen get into the blood?

You **breathe** air down into your **lungs**. The air contains oxygen. Your heart pumps blood to your lungs. Oxygen in your lungs goes into your blood. This blood, which now has a fresh supply of oxygen, travels back to your heart. Then the blood is pumped through your body so it can deliver oxygen to all parts of your body.

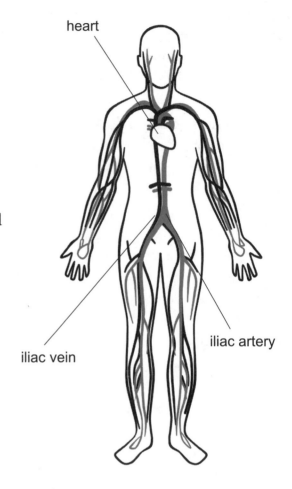

heart

iliac vein

iliac artery

Fun Facts

- If you took all the arteries, veins, and capillaries from an adult and laid them end to end, they would be long enough to go around the world two and a half times.
- In one tiny drop of blood, there are about 5 million red blood cells.
- A red blood cell dies after about four months. New red blood cells are made inside your bones.
- There is a lot of blood in your legs because gravity pulls the blood down. Since there is no gravity in outer space, astronauts on a space mission have less blood in their legs, and more blood in their chest and head.

"Your Cardiovascular System"—Think About It

1. This text is about the cardiovascular system. Explain why it is considered a system.

_____

_____

_____

2. Write one sentence to summarize each of the following sections of the text. Include only the most important ideas.

The Heart: _____

_____

Blood: _____

_____

Blood Vessels: _____

_____

Blood and Oxygen: _____

_____

3. What are three jobs that blood does in the body? Use specific details from the text to support your answer.

_____

_____

_____

4. What did you learn about capillaries from the diagram caption on page 23?

_____

_____

5. How many red blood cells are there in one tiny drop of blood? Where did you find that information in the text?

Are You Getting Enough ZZZs?

Eating good food and getting a lot of **exercise** are important to staying **healthy**. Getting enough **sleep** is important, too. Experts say that children between the ages of 5 and 12 need 10 to 11 hours of sleep each night.

Your body needs sleep for many reasons. It needs to take a **rest** from all the **activity** it has done during the day. Your brain needs a rest, too. You may not grow as well or you might get sick easier without enough sleep.

Your Body Clock

You have a **"24-hour clock"** inside your body that tells you when to be awake and when to go to sleep. This clock is controlled by your brain. **Blue light** that comes from the Sun tells your brain to keep you awake during the day. Then you can do all the things that you need to do. When there is no blue light at night, the brain tells the body it is time to go to sleep.

There are many things that stop the brain from telling your body when it is time to sleep. One of these is blue light at night. Today, people spend a lot of time watching **television** or looking at **screens** on **computers** or **smart phones**. These devices give off blue light. If you look at them at night, the blue light can trick your body into thinking it is daytime. Then it is harder to go to sleep and stay asleep.

What are some things that you can do to get a good night's sleep? Experts say that you should not look at screens that give off blue light for at least one hour before going to sleep. Two to three hours is better. Do not watch TV or use anything with a computer screen in bed. If you need to do something to fall asleep, it is better to read a book. Also, keep your bedroom as **dark** as you can. This will help your brain know it is time to sleep.

Fun Fact
Going to bed at the same time every night helps you get used to a schedule so you will be ready to sleep at the proper time.

"Are You Getting Enough ZZZs?"—Think About It

1. Name three things you can do to stay healthy.

_____

_____

_____

2. What does blue light do?

_____

_____

3. How do you think getting 10 hours of sleep a night could help someone your age?

_____

_____

_____

_____

4. Do you really have a 24-hour clock inside your body? Why do you think the author used the idea of a clock to describe what happens?

_____

_____

_____

_____

5. Do you think kids should have a regular bedtime? Explain your thinking.

_____

_____

_____

_____

More Vitamin C, Please

Humans cannot make their own **vitamin C**. People need to eat or drink food that contains vitamin C to get it into their bodies. **Oranges** and **orange juice** are one **source** of vitamin C. Read the following experiment to find out which type of orange juice had the most vitamin C.

What You Need
- 2% iodine solution
- cornstarch
- water
- eyedropper
- 2 small bowls
- measuring cup and spoons
- freshly squeezed orange juice
- orange juice made from frozen concentrate
- orange juice in a carton
- 3 test tubes
- small pot

What You Do
To make the vitamin C **indicator solution**:
1. In a small bowl, mix 1 tablespoon (15 ml) of cornstarch with enough water to make a paste.
2. Add 1 cup (250 ml) of water to the paste.
3. Put this into a small pot and boil for 5 minutes.
4. Measure 5 tbsp (75 ml) of water into another small bowl.
5. Use an eyedropper to add 10 drops of the cornstarch solution to the water.
6. Add the iodine solution to the water slowly until it turns a dark purple-blue color. This is your indicator solution.

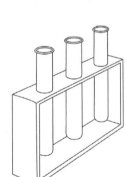

To test the orange juice:
1. Put 1 teaspoon (5 ml) of the indicator solution in each of the three test tubes.
2. Use an eyedropper to add 10 drops of juice to each of the test tubes: freshly squeezed orange juice in the first test tube, from frozen concentrate in the second test tube, and from a carton in the third. Clean the eyedropper for each sample.
3. Hold the test tubes against a white background. Line up the test tubes from the lightest color to the darkest.

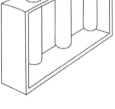

What Happened
The fresh orange juice was the lightest color. The orange juice from frozen concentrate was the next darkest. The orange juice from a carton was the darkest.

What You Need to Know
Vitamin C causes the indicator solution to lose color. The lighter the solution, the higher the vitamin C content.

"More Vitamin C, Please"—Think About It

1. Which orange juice had the most vitamin C? How do you know?

_____

_____

2. Why are the instructions under "What You Do" numbered? Why are numbers not used in "What You Need"?

_____

_____

_____

3. *Indicate* means to show or point out. What do you think the word *indicator* means? Why? What is an indicator solution?

_____

_____

_____

4. Why do you think the instructions say to hold the test tubes against a white background?

_____

_____

_____

5. Imagine you did the experiment. Draw a labeled diagram to show the result of Step 3 under "To test the orange juice."

Calories—We Need Them

Have you ever heard someone say "you do not need all those **calories**"? What does this mean? It does not mean that calories are bad for you. Calories are just a **measurement**. Calories tell you how much **energy** your body can get from food. Your body **burns** calories to get the energy it needs to do all its jobs. Your body burns calories to keep your heart and lungs working. It burns calories when you are doing your homework. It burns calories when you are walking. It even burns calories when you are sleeping.

But eating or drinking more calories than your body needs can cause problems. Calories that your body does not use are turned into **fat**. You need fat. Fat does many important jobs in your body. It **protects** organs such as the liver. It helps keep your body at the right temperature. It keeps your hair and skin healthy. It provides you with energy.

Too much fat though is not good for you. You can gain extra weight that you do not need if you eat too many calories. The **extra weight** can cause many **health problems** as you get older. One way to keep the right level of fat in your body is to get the right amount of calories your body needs.

You need some calories to give you energy for walking.

You need a lot of calories to give you energy to play active sports.

How Many Calories Do I Need?

The number of calories you need depends on many **factors**. One factor is your age. When children are growing, they need more calories. Another factor is how **active** you are. People who are very active (get a lot of exercise) burn more calories. People who are a little active (get some exercise, walk) need fewer calories. People who are not very active (spend most of their time sitting) need even fewer calories. Doctors and scientists have figured out the average number of calories needed by most people according to their age and activity level. Here are some guidelines for calories a young person needs.

Males			
Ages	**Not very active**	**Active**	**Very active**
10–11	1,700	2,000	2,300
12–13	1,900	2,250	2,600
14–16	2,300	2,700	3,100

Females			
Ages	**Not very active**	**Active**	**Very active**
10–11	1,500	1,800	2,050
12–13	1,700	2,000	2,250
14–16	1,750	2,100	2,350

Where Should I Get Calories From?

It is important to get the calories your body needs from many different foods. Foods have nutrients such as proteins, fats, carbohydrates, vitamins, minerals, and fiber. Your body needs all of these nutrients, but it needs them in the right amounts to stay healthy. You can find out what foods you should eat and how much you should eat by checking out a food guide. The United States has a food guide that can help you plan what you need to eat and drink every day.

Fun Facts

- 1 donut hole has the same number of calories as 19 grapes.
- 5 snack crackers have the same number of calories as 5.75 cups (1.4 liters) of cucumber slices.
- 1 chocolate chip cookie has the same number of calories as 53 chocolate-covered raisins.
- A person weighing 150 pounds (68 kg) would have to hike for 58 minutes to burn the calories in 1 chocolate brownie.
- A person weighing 150 pounds (68 kg) would have to vacuum the house for 85 minutes to burn the calories in a 20 ounce (590 ml) bottle of cola.

"Calories—We Need Them"—Think About It

1. What are calories?

_____

_____

2. Why is fat important for your body?

_____

_____

_____

_____

3. What is the main idea of the information under "How Many Calories Do I Need"?

_____

_____

4. What is the main idea of the information under "Where Should I Get Calories From?"

_____

_____

5. What is a food guide?

_____

_____

6. Explain the relationship between too much fat and your health.

_____

_____

_____

_____

"Calories—We Need Them"—Think About It (continued)

7. What does the text tell you about the difference in calories needed for boys and girls between the ages of 10 and 16?

8. What do the chart headings "Not very active," "Active," and "Very active" mean?

9. What advice would you give to someone about calories? Use information from the text and your own ideas.

10. List three facts from the Fun Facts box that were interesting to you.

Gluten and Lactose

Your **digestive system** has two main jobs:

- to turn the food you eat into **nutrients** your body needs
- to get rid of **waste** from food that your body does not need

Nutrients that you need are fats, proteins, carbohydrates, vitamins, minerals, and fiber. A **balanced diet** will give your body all of the nutrients it needs to keep you healthy and growing.

Sometimes the body does not work the way it should. This can happen when certain foods contain proteins or sugars that some people's bodies cannot digest.

Gluten

Gluten is a protein found in wheat, barley, and rye. Some people's bodies react negatively to that protein and they develop **celiac disease**. When they eat food with gluten, a **reaction** happens in their small intestines, or gut. This reaction **damages** the small intestine so it cannot take in nutrients from any food to the rest of the body.

People with celiac disease may have stomachaches and diarrhea. They may not want to eat and could lose weight. They may not grow the way they should. They could get a skin rash, too. These symptoms may come and go, depending on what they eat.

The best way for people to find out if they have celiac disease is to see a doctor. The good thing is that the disease can usually be controlled by not eating foods that contain gluten. Today there a many **gluten-free** products, and almost anything can be made without gluten by using a little imagination.

Lactose

Lactose is a type of natural sugar found in milk and other **dairy products**. Some people are **lactose intolerant**. This means their small intestines do not break down the lactose enough. When this undigested lactose moves into the large intestine, it can cause gas, pain or cramps, diarrhea, and throwing up. The best way for people to find out if they are lactose intolerant is to see a doctor.

Some people who are lactose intolerant cannot have any dairy products. Others can drink or eat small amounts without any problems. Like with celiac disease, the best thing to do is to not eat or drink any products that contain lactose.

Getting enough **calcium** can be a problem for young people who are lactose intolerant. But some **lactose-free** products contain calcium. Other foods that have calcium include broccoli, kale, salmon, almonds, fortified orange juice, and tofu.

"Gluten and Lactose"—Think About It

1. Why do you need a balanced diet?

_____

_____

2. What is this text describing?

_____

_____

3. What does the word *symptom* mean? How do you know?

_____

_____

4. What does *lactose intolerant* mean?

_____

5. Complete the following chart to compare and contrast what you learned about gluten and lactose.

	Gluten (celiac disease)	Lactose (lactose intolerant)
Foods it is found in	foods that contain wheat, barley, or rye	
Part of digestive system affected		small and large intestine
Symptoms	stomachaches, diarrhea, not wanting to eat, losing weight, not growing properly, skin rash	gas, pain or cramps, diarrhea, throwing up
Best way to treat	Do not eat foods that contain gluten	

6. Name three foods, other than milk or dairy products, that are rich in calcium.

_____

Read That Label!

Most people know what they are putting into their bodies when they eat a piece of chicken or a carrot. Food such as eggs, apples, and potatoes are called **natural foods**. There has been nothing added to the food before you cook it or eat it raw.

Foods that have other things added to them are called **processed foods**. Processed foods are usually found in a box, can, or bag. So how do you know what you are eating when you buy processed foods?

The Ingredient List

Processed foods have an ingredient list. This list tells you what is in the food. The ingredients are listed in the order of their weight. This means that the ingredient that weighs the most is listed first. The second ingredient by weight is listed next. Ingredients such as spices, flavorings, minerals, and vitamins are usually at the end of the list in any order. This is because they are small amounts.

Here is an example of an ingredient list from a cereal box:

Ingredients: Whole wheat, wheat bran, sugar/glucose-fructose, salt, malt (corn flour, malted barley), vitamins (thiamine hydrochloride, pyridoxine hydrochloride, folic acid, d-calcium pantothenate), minerals (iron, zinc oxide).

What Is in a Name?

Sometimes **fats**, **sodium**, and **sugar** are in an ingredient list under a different name. These are three things that most people want to know about because they do not want to eat too much of these ingredients. So it is important to know the other names of these common ingredients. Here are some examples of other names used:

- **Fat**: bacon, beef fat, butter, cocoa butter, lard, palm oil, shortening, suet, hard margarine, powdered whole milk
- **Sodium**: baking powder, baking soda, celery salt, garlic salt, monosodium glutamate (MSG), salt, sodium bisulfate, soy sauce
- **Sugar**: brown sugar, corn syrup, dextrose, fructose, glucose, high-fructose corn syrup, molasses, sucrose

Ingredient lists are also important because they can tell you if the food has something in it that you are allergic to or that makes you sick.

"Read That Label!"—Think About It

1. What is the difference between natural foods and processed foods?

_____

_____

2. a) What is the third ingredient in the cereal? What does this tell you about the amount of this ingredient in the cereal?

_____

_____

b) What else would you like to know about this ingredient to eat healthy?

_____

_____

3. Dextrose, fructose, glucose, and sucrose are all sugars. What do all these words have in common? What do you think the word _maltose_ means? Why?

_____

_____

_____

4. What is the main idea of the information under "The Ingredient List"? What is the main idea of the information under "What Is in a Name?"

_____

_____

_____

5. We need a small amount of sodium to keep healthy. Too much sodium can cause health problems. Salt is made from sodium and chloride. Explain the relationship between a healthy body and too much salt.

_____

_____

_____

Mysteries of Stonehenge

A Very Strange Structure

In an open field in England, there is a strange group of **stone blocks** known as **Stonehenge**. Thousands of years ago, the blocks formed the **structure**.

Today, some of the stones have fallen over. Other stones are missing because they were removed long ago to be used to build new structures. What makes Stonehenge a mystery? There are two questions scientists have been trying to answer:

1. How did people build Stonehenge thousands of years ago without the tools and machines we have today?
2. Why did people build Stonehenge?

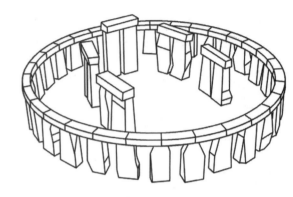

Stonehenge reconstruction

How Was Stonehenge Built?

The blocks in Stonehenge are huge. The largest blocks weigh about 40 tons (36 **tonnes**). When Stonehenge was built, the **wheel** had not yet been invented. Then how did the builders move the blocks to that site? Some experts believe that logs were used under the stones to act like rollers. The rolling logs made the blocks much easier to drag.

The next challenge was to place the **standing stones** in an upright position. One theory is the builders first dug a **hole** in the spot where the stone was to be placed. They then **tipped** the stone so the bottom of it fell into the hole, and used **ropes** to pull the stone upright. When the stone was upright, the builders filled in the hole with dirt to support the stone.

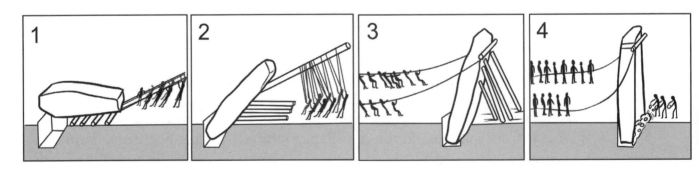

Steps for moving a standing stone into place

Mysteries of Stonehenge (continued)

The toughest job of all was to place the stones that sit on top of the standing stones. (These top stones are called **lintels**.) It is possible that the builders created dirt **ramps** beside the standing stones, then built a **wooden track** on top of the ramp. They could then drag the lintels up the wooden track and into place. The people could then remove the ramp when they were finished.

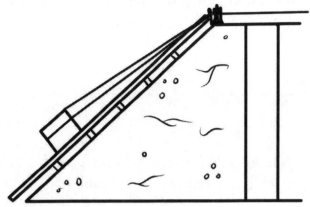

Lintel being pulled up a ramp

On top of the standing stones, the workers carved out small round bumps. On the bottom of the lintels, they created small holes. When they placed the lintels on the standing stones, the bumps fit into the holes to hold the lintels in place. They also cut special **mortise** and **tenon joints** in the ends of the stones. Those joints made the stones fit together like puzzle pieces.

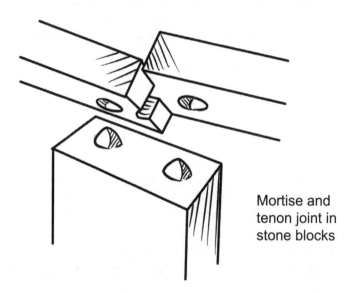

Mortise and tenon joint in stone blocks

Why Was Stonehenge Built?

The question of why people built Stonehenge is the biggest mystery of all. Over the years, experts have suggested many different ideas. Here are some examples:

1. Stonehenge was like a huge clock that helped people to mark the seasons. For example, on the longest day of year (in summer) and the shortest day (in winter), people stood inside Stonehenge and watched the sun rise. On these days, the sun was visible in the space between certain standing stones.
2. Stonehenge was a place where people went to worship ancient gods.
3. Stonehenge was built as a place to bury the dead. Graves have been found around the site.

We will probably never know for sure how and why Stonehenge was built. The answers to those mysteries are buried deep in the past.

"Mysteries of Stonehenge"—Think About It

1. It is amazing that some parts of Stonehenge are still standing. What three natural forces do you think that Stonehenge has had to withstand over thousands of years?

a) _____

b) _____

c) _____

2. Workers might have used simple machines to build Stonehenge. How might the following simple machines have been used? (Hint: Look at the illustrations.)

a) An inclined plane (a slanting surface)

_____

_____

_____

b) A lever (a stiff bar used to move a load)

_____

_____

_____

3. Why do you think Stonehenge was built? Choose one of the theories in the text or make up your own. Give a reason why you think it is the best theory.

_____

_____

_____

_____

_____

_____

_____

The Hoover Dam

The Hoover Dam is one of the tallest dams in the world. No wonder more than a million people visit the dam each year.

Flood Control, Power, and More

The Hoover Dam is located in the Black Canyon on the Colorado River. The dam is in the southwestern United States, on the border between Arizona and Nevada.

The dam was built to control floods and to create a reservoir, or a place to store water. This reservoir is called Lake Mead. It is the largest reservoir in the United States. The water at the Hoover Dam and Lake Mead is also used to power machines that make electricity that is called hydroelectric power.

Before Construction

There were no towns in Colorado near the site where the Hoover Dam was to be built. So before work could begin on the dam, houses had to be built nearby so the construction workers had places to live. The town became known as Boulder City.

A highway to the site also had to be built. As well, a railroad was extended to the site so that supplies could easily be brought in.

In 1931, construction finally began on the Hoover Dam.

Building Begins

Building the dam was difficult and, in the summers, the sun could be scorching. No structure this big had ever been built out of concrete.

The dam is built in columns of huge, concrete blocks. About 215 of these blocks were locked together, then cemented in place. There is enough concrete in the dam to pave a standard size highway all the way across the country from San Francisco to New York City. Experts say the Hoover Dam weighs more than 6,600,000 tons (5,987,419 tonnes).

A total of 21,000 construction workers were needed to build the dam. Some days, more than 5,200 were hard at work. They handled huge amounts of reinforcement steel, pipes, valves, gates, and more. Sadly, more than 100 men died constructing the dam, either due to falls or other accidents.

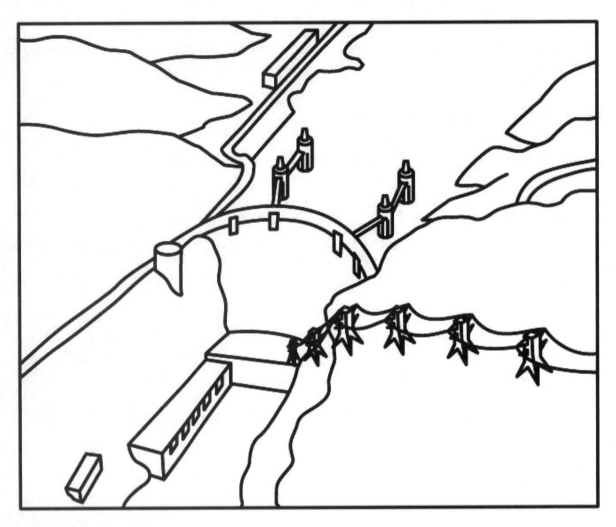

Construction Complete

The dam was completed on March 1, 1936. It was originally known as the Boulder Dam. In 1947, it was renamed after Herbert Hoover, who was the American president when the dam-building began.

At more than seven stories high, Hoover Dam was one of the largest human-made structures in the world when it was built. It was also one of the largest producers of hydroelectricity.

Fun Facts

- There are 17 generators at the Hoover Dam. Each generator can supply electricity to 100,000 homes.
- The base of the Hoover Dam is 660 ft. (201 m) thick. It measures the same as two football fields placed end to end.
- About 20,000 vehicles per day drive across the 45 ft. (14 m) wide top of the dam between Nevada and Arizona.

"Hoover Dam"—Think About It

1. Putting dams in rivers changes the water flow and the environment for animals and plants. Do you think building dams is a good idea? Explain your thinking.

_____

_____

_____

2. How is the Hoover Dam used? Use details from the text to support your answer.

_____

_____

3. This dam was named Boulder Dam, then changed to Hoover Dam. Why did the name change?

_____

_____

4. Would you like to visit the Hoover Dam? Why or why not?

_____

_____

_____

5. How many people visit the Hoover Dam on average every year?

_____

6. What is the biggest structure or building you have ever seen? What impressed you about it?

_____

_____

_____

7. When was the Hoover Dam completed?

_____

Famous Bridges

Bridges are **structures**. They are built across rivers, valleys, seas, and even across roads and railways. Bridges help move people and vehicles from one side of something to the other side.

Early bridges were made from stone or wood. There are still bridges built today from these materials because they are not very expensive and the bridges are easier to build. But most new bridges are built from **steel** and **concrete**.

There are many different types of bridges, including **arch bridges**, **beam bridges**, and **suspension bridges.**

Arch Bridges

Arch bridges have been built for hundreds of years. The **Romans** were famous for building them. Arches give this bridge its strength. Arch bridges can be built from many materials including wood, stone, concrete, or steel. A bridge can have one or many arches. One famous arch bridge is the **Peace Bridge**. This is an international bridge between the United States and Canada. It connects Fort Erie, Ontario, with Buffalo, New York. It has five arches.

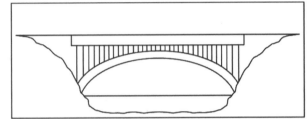

Beam Bridges

Simple beam bridges are the oldest known bridges—even older than arch bridges. They have vertical **pilings** and horizontal **beams**. The road is built on the horizontal beams. Beam bridges can be made very long by adding more vertical pilings. **Lake Pontchartrain Causeway** in Louisiana is a famous beam bridge. It is really 2, two-lane bridges side by side. It is 22 miles (39 km) long and has over 9,000 pilings.

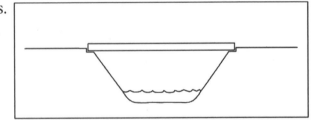

Suspension Bridges

Suspension bridges are strong and can span long distances. They are usually found across **harbors**. Suspension bridges have steel **cables** that stretch over two **towers**. These cables are attached at each end of the bridge to an **anchor**. Smaller cables are attached to the big cables at one end and the road at the other. They help support the road. The **Golden Gate Bridge** in San Francisco, California, is a famous suspension bridge. It opened in 1937. At night, it is lit with lights and looks very beautiful.

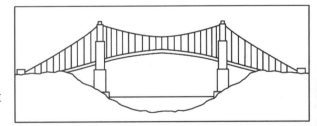

"Famous Bridges"—Think About It

1. How many lanes does the Lake Pontchartrain Causeway have?

_____

_____

2. Which type of bridge do you think is the newest type of bridge? Why?

_____

3. Draw the diagram of a beam bridge below. Label the pilings and the road. Where are the horizontal beams? What does *vertical* mean? What does *horizontal* mean?

_____

_____

4. One meaning of *suspended* is to hang something from somewhere, for example, to suspend a light from the ceiling. Why do you think suspension bridges are called that?

_____

_____

_____

5. The Peace Bridge is an international bridge. What does this mean?

_____

_____

Why Igloos Work

Inuit people are the **original** inhabitants of North America's Arctic region. They are a very **strong** people. They have to be because the Arctic is a very **difficult** place to live. Inuit live mostly in the **tundra**. The tundra has few plants and trees.

In the past, Inuit ate mostly animals. They lived in tent-like **huts** made from animal skins in the summer. In the winter, they traveled farther north to the sea ice to hunt for seals. They also hunted whales, walruses, and polar bears. In their winter camps, they built and lived in **igloos**. They might stay in an igloo for a few days or for the whole winter.

Why were igloos good winter homes?

- Igloos are made from snow blocks. There is a lot of snow in the Arctic in the winter so Inuit always had the material they needed to build an igloo.

- All you need to build an igloo is a saw or a large knife and a shovel. Someone who knows how to build an igloo can build a small one in less than an hour.

- Igloos are shaped like a **dome**. Domes are like half a sphere. A structure in the shape of a dome is very strong. Domes also support their own weight. They do not need walls or columns inside to hold them up.

- The walls of an igloo block the wind. It is very windy in the Arctic, and it can make the **temperature** feel much colder. The tightly packed snow blocks stop freezing winds from reaching the people inside the igloo.

- Snow and ice act as an **insulator**. This means that heat inside the igloo stays there. Any heat made inside the igloo does not escape. Temperatures inside an igloo can be much warmer than outside.

- Igloos can be big or small. They can be built for one person or for a whole family. Some can be big enough to use as a meeting hall.

Today, most Inuit live in **permanent communities** all year round. But many still build igloos today when they go on hunting trips.

"Why Igloos Work"—Think About It

1. What was the difference between Inuit summer homes and winter homes?

_____

_____

2. The text says that Inuit traveled north to the sea ice to hunt seals. What does this tell you about seals?

_____

_____

_____

3. What was the relationship between the food Inuit ate and where they lived?

_____

_____

4. Write a summary explaining why igloos are good winter homes.

_____

_____

_____

_____

5. What does the word _insulator_ mean? How do you know?

_____

_____

_____

6. How does the author organize the information to answer the question "Why were igloos good winter homes"? How does this help you understand the information?

_____

_____

_____

_____

How Buildings Kill Birds

Every year, millions of birds in North America are **killed** or **injured** when they fly into **buildings**. Why does this happen? The answer is **glass**. Birds are flying into windows and tall buildings that are entirely covered by glass.

The Daytime Danger of Glass

Many birds **migrate** from one place to another. Most of the time, these birds live in wild habitats, such as forests, meadows, and wetlands. These birds have no idea what glass is. They might see small trees and flowers inside a window and think these **plants** will provide them with a good place to take a rest. The birds have no idea that there is a sheet of clear glass between them and the plants, so the birds end up flying right into the glass.

In some cities, there are many buildings covered with **mirrored glass**. A low building covered with mirrored glass might **reflect** an image of the park across the street. On a skyscraper, mirrored glass might reflect the image of a clear **blue sky**. Birds do not understand that these images are only reflections, so they fly right into the glass.

The Nighttime Danger of Glass

Some birds fly at night as they migrate long distances. Many of these birds use the **moon** and **stars** to help guide them in the right **direction**. Tall buildings that leave lights on at night can confuse the birds. This is a big problem on **foggy** and **rainy** nights. The birds see the light, but they cannot tell that the light is coming from inside a building. Their instinct is to fly toward the light, so they end up crashing into a building.

On many mornings, there might be several dead birds lying at the bottom of an office tower that keeps its lights on at night. The building's **janitors** remove the dead birds long before people start arriving for work, so many people do not even know about the problem.

Trying to Solve the Problem

Many office buildings now turn off their lights at night. This helps **reduce** the number of birds that fly into buildings, and it also helps save **energy**.

48

"How Buildings Kill Birds"—Think About It

1. There are two paragraphs under the subheading The Daytime Danger of Glass. Write one sentence to summarize the most important information in each paragraph.

First paragraph: _____
_____
_____

Second paragraph: _____
_____
_____

2. Why are the moon and stars important to birds that migrate at night?

_____
_____
_____

3. How can a migrating bird's instincts get the bird into danger when it flies through a city at night?

_____
_____
_____

4. Why are many people unaware that birds are killed by flying into office buildings at night?

_____
_____
_____

5. What are two benefits of turning off the lights in office buildings at night?

_____
_____
_____

How Does That Fly?

What Forces Affect Airplanes?

Airplanes fly because of four **forces**. These forces are **weight**, **lift**, **thrust**, and **drag**.

- Weight is the force of **gravity** on the plane. Gravity wants to pull the plane down toward Earth.
- Lift is the force that acts to keep the plane up. Lift is created by the differences in **air pressure** below the wings of a plane and above the wings.
- Thrust is the force that moves the plane **forward**. Engines of a plane produce thrust.
- Drag is the force that wants to pull the plane **backward**. Drag is caused by **friction** between the body of the plane and the air.

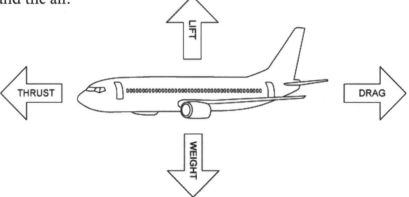

For an airplane to **take off**, the thrust must be greater than the drag, and the lift must be greater than the weight. For an airplane to land, the thrust must be less than the drag, and the lift must be less than the weight. When the airplane is **flying straight** and at an even level, thrust and drag are equal, and lift and weight are equal.

Bigger and Bigger Planes

Since the first flight in a powered, **controlled** airplane in 1903, planes have gotten bigger and bigger. The airplane that first made **air travel** popular and profitable was the Douglas DC-3. Introduced in 1936, this plane could carry 21 passengers and fly 1,494 mi. (2,405 km) non-stop. Today, the Airbus A380 can carry 525 passengers and fly 9,756 mi. (15,700 km) non-stop. Why can planes get so much bigger and still fly?

Bigger planes need engines that produce more speed. The invention of the **jet engine** allowed planes to fly faster and higher. **Commercial jet planes** started flying in the 1950s. Through the years, jet engines have become **more powerful** so planes can fly faster. They have also become more **fuel efficient**. The faster a plane can fly, the more lift it will have. But weight is still important, especially when the planes are bigger and they carry more passengers. Airplane makers have done many things to keep their planes as light as possible. The bodies of airplanes are being made of materials that are **lighter** and yet **strong**. Even seats are being made of lighter materials.

"How Does That Fly?"—Think About It

1. What does gravity want to do to an airplane? What does drag want to do? What two forces overcome gravity and drag so a plane can fly?

_____

_____

2. Which part of the text does the diagram relate to? Does the diagram help you understand the written information better? Why or why not?

_____

_____

_____

3. What happens to the forces when an airplane is flying level and straight?

_____

_____

4. One meaning of the word *efficient* is to use a product with the least waste or effort. What do you think the phrase "fuel efficient" means?

_____

_____

_____

5. Why are jet engines important for modern planes?

_____

_____

_____

6. What are the differences between the first passenger airplanes and the planes today?

_____

_____

_____

Fill It Up!

Most cars, trucks, buses, and motorcycles run on **gasoline**. There are vehicles today that use **alternative fuels**. These are fuels that can be used in place of gasoline. They include

- **ethanol** (made from corn)
- **biodiesel** (made from soybean oil, vegetable oil, animal fats, or recycled cooking oil)
- **compressed natural gas** (natural gas that has been squeezed so it takes up less space)

There are also vehicles that run on **electricity** or on a combination of electricity and another fuel.

Still, gasoline-powered vehicles are the most common. Where does gasoline come from and how does it get to a vehicle?

From the Ground to Your Car

Gasoline comes from **crude oil**. Crude oil is also called **petroleum**. Usually, crude oil is found in the ground as a liquid. To get the oil, a hole is drilled to the oil. Then it is pumped out of the ground.

Crude oil is made up of **hydrocarbons**. There are many different types of hydrocarbons in crude oil, so it has to be **refined** first. During the refining process, the crude oil is heated. The different hydrocarbons turn into a **vapor** (a gas) at different temperatures. So during refining, the different hydrocarbons are separated from each other.

Here is a list of some of the hydrocarbons that come from crude oil: butane, propane, gasoline, diesel, kerosene, asphalt, and tar. Each of these has different uses.

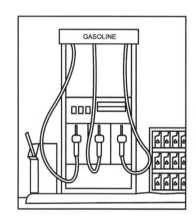

Once gasoline is refined, **chemicals** are added. These chemicals help make a vehicle run better by doing things such as cleaning the engine. Sometimes gasoline is further refined so some chemicals do not need to be added.

When the gasoline is ready, it is usually transported to a **terminal**. **Pipelines** are most often used to do this. The terminal is a big **storage** place. **Tanker trucks** fill up at these terminals. They carry the gasoline to gas stations, where the gasoline is stored in large tanks underground. The pumps at a gas station pump out the gasoline from the tanks into the vehicles.

"Fill It Up!"—Think About It

1. What is this text about? Write a two-sentence summary to answer this question.

_____

_____

2. What is another name for crude oil? What does crude oil contain?

_____

_____

3. What fuels can be used to make vehicles run?

_____

_____

_____

4. Draw a flow chart to show the process of getting gasoline from the ground to a vehicle.

5. What does _compressed_ mean? How do you know?

_____

_____

Geothermal Electricity

Creating Electricity

Most of the **electricity** people use is generated at places called **power plants**. Electricity is created when **magnets** spin inside a generator at the power plant. The magnets spin because they are connected to a **turbine** that spins. It takes energy to make the turbine spin.

There are different ways to make a turbine spin. Some power plants use the energy of **moving water** to make a turbine spin. **Steam** can also make a turbine spin. In a **coal** power plant, heat from burning coal is used to turn water into steam. Some power plants burn **oil** to turn water to steam. Burning coal or oil puts **pollution** into the air.

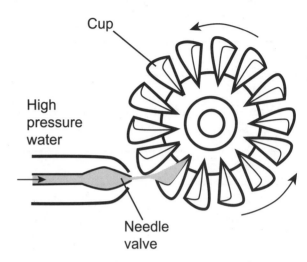

Cup

High pressure water

Needle valve

A typical Pelton water turbine. Water is directed into the turbine cups, making it spin.

Geothermal Power Plants

In some places, there are power plants that use **water** from a **reservoir**, or pool, that is deep **underground**. This water is already very hot, so there is no need to heat the water to create steam. These power plants are called **geothermal power plants**. (See the diagram on the next page.)

Geo means "from the Earth" and *thermal* means "heat." A geothermal power plant uses water that is heated by Earth. How does this happen? Deep inside Earth, the **temperature** is hot enough to **melt** rock. We see this melted rock when a volcano erupts. The lava that comes out of a volcano is molten, or melted, rock.

Water that is deep underground is heated by Earth. At a geothermal power plant, pipes **pump** hot water from 1.2 to 1.9 mi. (2 or 3 km) underground. At the surface of Earth, the hot water turns to steam. The steam makes a turbine spin. The spinning turbine makes magnets in the generator spin. The spinning magnets generate electricity.

Once the steam has passed by the turbine, the steam goes to a **cooling tower**. As the steam cools, it **condenses** back into water. Then the water travels through a pipe that takes it back underground. The Earth heats the water again, so the geothermal power plant can use the same water over and over again.

Geothermal Electricity (continued)

How a Geothermal Power Plant Works

1. Hot water is pumped from a reservoir deep underground.
2. The hot water turns to steam.
3. Steam makes the turbine spin. The turbine makes magnets spin inside the generator. Electricity is created.
4. Steam condenses into water at the cooling tower.
5. The water goes back underground, where it is heated again.

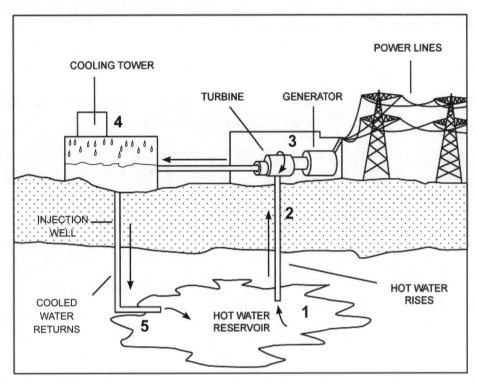

Benefits of Geothermal Power Plants

Most people who are worried about the **environment** think geothermal power plants are a good idea. One reason is that geothermal power plants do not pollute the air by burning coal or oil to change water to steam. Another reason is that the hot underground water that geothermal power plants use is a **renewable resource**. The water goes back underground, so it is not used up. Coal and oil are not renewable resources.

Fun Facts

- In Iceland, 25% of the country's total electricity is generated by geothermal power.
- In 1904, Italy became the first country to use geothermal power to create electricity.
- Farmers in Italy have used geothermal energy for hundreds of years to heat water for winter crops.
- In the western United States, including Hawaii, geothermal thermal energy sources are closer to Earth's surface. There are many geothermal power plants on the west coast of the United States.
- In the United States, geothermal energy is also used to melt snow and ice on sidewalks and roads. This saves communities money that would normally be spent on snowplows and salt trucks and the fossil fuels they use.
- Although geothermal energy is a very clean energy source, there are some solid waste products left over. Zinc and sulphur are waste minerals left from the process that need to be disposed of or sold.

"Geothermal Electricity"—Think About It

1. What does the word *generated* mean?

_____

2. Below are two main ideas from the first part of the text. For each main idea, write two details from the text that help to explain the main idea.

Main idea: Most electricity is generated at power plants.
Main idea: There are different ways to make a turbine spin.

3. Niagara Falls is the name for three waterfalls on the border of the United States and Canada. Both countries have built power plants at Niagara Falls. Why is this a good place for power plants?

_____

_____

_____

"Geothermal Electricity"—Think About It (continued)

4. What is the name of the pipe that carries the water back underground at a geothermal power plant? Tell how you know.

5. What reasons does the author give to explain why many people who care about the environment like the idea of geothermal power plants?

6. Do you think using geothermal energy is a good idea? Why or why not?

Power from the Wind

Wind turbines are large **windmills** that produce **energy**. As wind moves the **blades** of a wind turbine, **electricity** is produced. Read the two texts about wind turbines.

Letter to the Editor

More and more people today are realizing that we need to stop relying so much on getting energy from oil and coal. Using these **fossil fuels** causes **pollution** that leads to climate change.

How do we get energy if we do not use fossil fuels? I often hear people talk about building more **nuclear power** plants and getting energy from the **Sun** by using solar panels. These are good **alternatives**, but there is an excellent alternative that people do not seem to talk about as much—using **wind turbines** to **generate electricity**.

Throughout history, people have used wind power. Sailboats get power from the wind, and people have been using sailboats for centuries. **Windmills** have also been around for centuries, and they use power from the wind to **pump water** or **grind grain** into flour. Today's wind turbines are a type of windmill that uses wind power to generate electricity.

In my opinion, we need more wind turbines. They do not use up fossil fuels, and wind is a **renewable** source of energy—we will never run out of wind. The other benefit of wind turbines is that they do not create pollution, so they do not contribute to climate change.

I encourage everyone to learn more about wind turbines, and to ask government officials to build more wind turbines. Wind power is a great way to generate **clean energy** and use less fossil fuel.

Leon Jones

Blog Entry

Welcome to Kerry's Blog!   Today is January 12.

So what is the story on wind energy? I have been
doing some research. Wind turbines seem to
be a pretty good way to produce energy. They
do not pollute the air, they are cheaper to build
than power-generating plants, and they do not
use up fossil fuels, which are **non-renewable
resources**. I found out that some people do not
like wind turbines. I am going to tell you some
of the problems they point out, and my thoughts
on each problem.

Problem 1: Birds are killed when they fly into wind turbines.
Okay, that makes sense, but my research tells me that more birds are killed
each year by flying into tall buildings that keep their lights on at night. A huge
number of birds are killed each year by pet cats that people let wander outside.
In comparison, the number of birds killed by wind turbines is low. If we want to
save birds, let us look after the bigger problems first.

Problem 2: Wind turbines produce energy only on windy days.
Yes, that is true. But no one is talking about using only wind turbines to produce
energy. We do need to have other sources of energy to use on days when there is
no wind. Wind turbines can help us reduce the amount of pollution that other
energy sources put into the air. Also, wind turbines can help us use less energy
from non-renewable sources.

Problem 3: Wind turbines make too much noise.
Noise can be a problem when we build wind turbines in areas where people live
and work. We do not have to build wind turbines in those places. There is a lot
of open land in North America where wind turbines would not bother anyone.
I also found out that people are working to design wind turbines that are much
quieter.

Wind turbines might not be perfect, but they are still a good idea!

"Power from the Wind"—Think About It

1. Leon and Kerry both think wind turbines are a good idea, but their points of view on the issue are not exactly the same. How are they different?

_____

_____

_____

_____

_____

2. What points do both Leon and Kerry make to support the idea of wind turbines?

_____

_____

_____

_____

_____

3. List two specific benefits of wind turbines that are mentioned by only one of the writers. Name the writer who mentioned each benefit.

Benefit	Writer

"Power from the Wind"—Think About It (continued)

4. Kerry points out three problems with wind turbines. For which problem does she not offer a solution?

_____

_____

_____

5. Which text do you think would be most likely to persuade readers to support wind power? Tell why.

_____

_____

_____

_____

_____

_____

_____

_____

_____

_____

6. Do you think using wind power is a good idea? Why or why not?

_____

_____

_____

_____

_____

_____

_____

When Water Changes State

The hummingbird flew to the feeder and put its tongue into the small hole. What it wanted was the sugar and water solution inside. But no luck today. The solution was **frozen**. It had changed from a liquid to a solid overnight because of the **cold temperature**. When that happens, most hummingbirds will **migrate** south to warmer places.

States of Matter

Matter can be found in three **states: gas**, **liquid**, and **solid**. Some matter, such as water, can change from one state to another because of changes in temperature.

Changes in the state of matter can cause **problems** for people as well. **Black ice** forms when water suddenly turns into ice on roads and sidewalks. Black ice should really be called "clear ice" because it freezes with few air bubbles. This makes it transparent. What you see is the road under the ice. Black ice makes roads look as though they are wet.

Black ice can be very dangerous. For example, stopping on black ice can take a car nine times longer than normal. There are things people can do to make driving on black ice safer. Most important is to make sure the vehicle is in top condition. Driving slower than usual can help, too. In some places, sand is put on the ice. This gives the tires a better surface to stick to. In other places, salt is used. **Salt** lowers the freezing temperature of ice and can change it back into a liquid.

Problems can also happen when water changes from a liquid to a gas. This is called **evaporation**. Evaporation of water can happen at any temperature. But water will evaporate very quickly when it boils, but hardly at all when it gets close to freezing.

Reservoirs are used to store large amounts of water. Water in a reservoir is used for many things. It can be used to make electricity, for **irrigating** farmland, and for home and business use. Reservoirs lose a lot of water through evaporation. One way to stop this is to put a special cover over the water. Scientists are working on other ways to stop evaporation because **saving water** is very important.

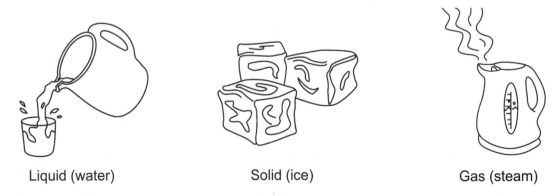

Liquid (water)   Solid (ice)   Gas (steam)

"When Water Changes State"—Think About It

1. Why did the solution in the hummingbird feeder freeze?

_____

_____

2. Why is salt put on black ice?

_____

_____

3. How are temperature and evaporation of water related?

_____

_____

_____

4. Subheadings can help a reader understand a text better. Where might subheadings appear in this text that would help a reader? What main idea could these heading be about?

_____

_____

_____

5. a) What does the word *transparent* mean? How do you know?

_____

_____

b) Name one other thing that is transparent.

_____

6. What is the relationship between evaporation and reservoirs?

_____

_____

_____

What Is a Landfill?

A **landfill** is a place where **garbage** is buried. Some landfills are holes in the ground, and some are hills of garbage on top of the ground. The diagram below shows a landfill built in a hole in the ground.

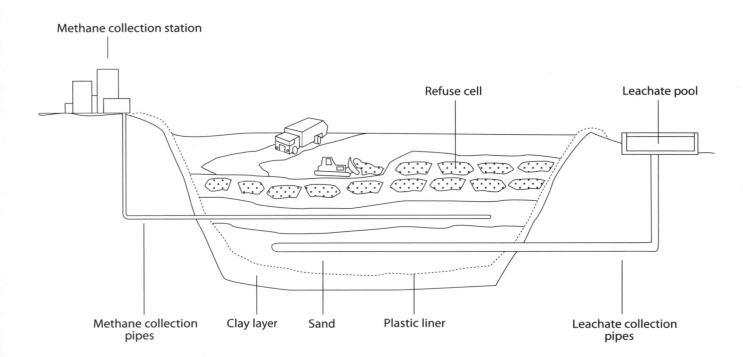

Each day, trucks dump loads of garbage in the landfill. At the end of each day, all the garbage from the day is covered with a layer of dirt. One day's garbage covered with dirt is called a **refuse cell**. (Refuse, which is another word for garbage, is pronounced like this: *ref-yooz*).

When it rains on a landfill, the **rainwater** seeps down through all the garbage. Rainwater that seeps through a landfill is called **leachate**. It is important to keep the leachate from seeping into the soil under the landfill. There might be dangerous **chemicals** in the landfill that go into the leachate. The leachate can **pollute** the soil, and it can also pollute water that is underground. Then the polluted underground water might end up in a well that someone uses to get drinking water. The polluted water might also go into a lake or river that provides a community with drinking water.

Dealing with Leachate

Most landfills have three features to keep leachate from mixing with soil and water under the landfill:

Leachate collection pipes: Directly under the bottom of the landfill are pipes that are surrounded by a layer of sand. There are many small holes in the pipes. Leachate flows through the sand and collects in the pipes. The leachate then flows into pipes that do not have holes. These pipes carry the leachate to a place where any dangerous chemicals can be removed.

Plastic liner: Under the leachate collection pipes and sand, there is a plastic liner. This liner prevents leachate from seeping down into the soil.

Clay barrier: It is possible that the plastic liner might develop a hole that allows leachate to leak through. The clay barrier provides an extra layer of protection. Clay can absorb and hold onto a lot of water. If some leachate does leak through the liner, the clay barrier keeps the leachate from seeping down into the soil under the landfill.

Once a landfill can hold no more garbage, it is **covered** over with dirt. Then grass and trees are **planted** on top. Some landfills become **parks** or **sports fields**.

The Problem with Landfills

A city produces large amounts of garbage year after year. Most landfills take up a lot of land so they can hold a lot of garbage. Once a landfill can hold no more garbage, a new landfill must be created. Many communities are running out of **space** for new landfills. A community might need empty land for building new houses or factories, or for farmland.

Landfills are one reason why **recycling** is important. When people recycle, less of their garbage ends up in landfills. Then fewer landfills are needed.

Fun Facts

- The average North American will throw away 600 times their adult weight in garbage in their lifetime. This means a 150 lb. (68 kg) adult will throw away 89,949 lb. (40,800 kg) of garbage during their life.
- It takes 10 plastic soda bottles to make the warm lining for one ski jacket.
- 1 lb. (450 g) of newspaper can be recycled to make 6 egg cartons, 6 cereal boxes, or 2,000 sheets of paper.
- 70% of the garbage in landfill sites could be reused or recycled.
- Americans use about 102.1 billion plastic bags each year, creating tons (tonnes) of landfill waste.
- Each year, 38,000 mi. of ribbon are thrown away. That is enough to tie a bow around Earth.

"What Is a Landfill?"—Think About It

1. Here is one main idea in the text: Many communities are running out of space for new landfills. Write two details from the text that support this main idea.

_____

_____

_____

2. Write a definition of the word _barrier_. (Do not define the clay barrier in the text. Write a definition that would fit any type of barrier.)

_____

_____

_____

3. The text says that it is important to keep the leachate from seeping into the soil under the landfill. What reasons does the author give to support this statement?

_____

_____

_____

4. How does the clay barrier help to protect the soil under a landfill?

_____

_____

_____

5. How can a landfill site that is full help to benefit a community? Explain your thinking.

_____

_____

6. Why are fewer landfills needed when people recycle? Explain your thinking.

_____

_____

The Dinofish

The year was 1938. Marjorie Courtenay-Latimer was working in a tiny **museum** in the town of East London on the coast of South Africa. As part of her job, Marjorie collected **natural objects** such as shells, feathers, and rocks to **display** in the museum.

Marjorie thought it would be a good idea to add some **unusual fish** to the museum's collection. She had alerted fishers in the area to let her know if they caught any unusual fish.

An Early Christmas Gift

On December 3, Marjorie got a phone call asking if she wanted to come to the docks to look at the fish that had been caught that day. Marjorie almost did not go. She was busy preparing a display of **reptiles** for the museum. Then she decided that, since it was getting close to Christmas, she would go to the docks just to wish the fishers a happy holiday.

Beautiful Fish

Down at the docks, Marjorie chatted with the fishers and wished them a merry Christmas. She was just about to leave when she happened to glance down at a pile of fish that had been unloaded from a boat. She noticed an **unusual fin** sticking out of the pile. Curious, she pushed aside the fish lying on top and saw what she described as "the most beautiful fish I had ever seen." The fish was blue, about 5 ft. (1.5 m) long, and had silver markings on its body. Marjorie had never seen a fish like that before. She wanted to preserve it to display in the museum.

Strange New Species

When she got back to the museum with the strange fish, Marjorie looked through books to try to identify it. Finally, she found a drawing of a fish called a **coelacanth** (say it like this: *seel-uh-kanth*) that looked very similar to the one she had found. There was just one problem—the coelacanth was known only from **fossils**. Scientists believed the fish had become **extinct** about 65 million years ago, around the same time that **dinosaurs** disappeared.

Coelacanth is a large fish with limblike fins, armored scales, and a tail unlike any other living fish.

Exciting Discovery!

Marjorie made a quick drawing of the fish and sent it to James Smith, a fish **expert** she knew. He was away at the time but, on January 3, 1939, Marjorie got a **telegram** from him. James was very excited about Marjorie's fish. He said he would travel to East London as soon as he could. He arrived at the museum on February 16 and confirmed that the fish really was a coelacanth.

Front Page News!

A newspaper **reporter** took a picture of the fish. Soon the picture appeared in **newspapers** around the world. Everyone was amazed that a fish people believed had died out millions of years **ago** had **survived** deep in the ocean. Marjorie became famous, and the coelacanth was called the most important animal **discovery of the century**.

Fun Facts

- After Marjorie's discovery, a reward was offered to anyone who could catch a second coelacanth. Fourteen years passed before another coelacanth was caught.
- Coelacanths appear to stand on their head. They sometimes float with their head pointing down and their tail pointing up.
- Scientists believe that coelacanths live for about 60 years in the wild, although some may live much longer.
- There are only two species of coelacanths known to scientists. One species of coelacanth lives near the Comoro Islands off the east coast of Africa. Another species of coelacanth was found in the waters off Sulawesi, Indonesia.
- Coelacanths are considered an endangered species.
- Coelacanths live in depths up to 2,297 ft. (700 m) below the surface.

"The Dinofish"—Think About It

1. "Dinofish" is a nickname some people use for the coelacanth. Why would people choose this nickname?

_____

_____

2. Is the overall structure of this text problem and solution, chronology, or cause and effect? Explain your answer.

_____

_____

3. Give two reasons why Marjorie almost did not discover the coelacanth.

_____

_____

_____

4. What steps did Marjorie take to identify the strange fish she had found?

_____

_____

_____

_____

5. How do you know that people have observed live coelacanths in their natural habitat?

_____

_____

6. Do you agree that the discovery of the coelacanth was the most important animal discovery of the century? Explain your thinking.

_____

_____

_____

Discovering King Tut's Tomb

Who Was King Tut?

King Tut's real name was **Tutankhamen**. He was a
pharaoh in ancient Egypt. A pharaoh was a ruler, like a
king, in ancient Egypt. Tutankhamen lived a short life—
he died when he was just 18 or 19 years old. While he is
famous today, few people in the modern world had heard
about Tutankhamen before his **tomb** was discovered in
1922.

Tombs in the Valley of the Kings

Archaeologists learn about **history** by finding and
studying objects from the past. Many archaeologists
worked in the Valley of the Kings, an area in Egypt
where Egyptian pharaohs were buried in ancient times.
Over centuries, these tombs had been covered by sand.
Archaeologists digging in the sand had discovered the
tombs of many pharaohs.

By the early 1900s, most archaeologists believed that
there were no more tombs to be found in the Valley of
the Kings. One archaeologist named Howard Carter did
not agree. He believed that the tomb of Tutankhamen
was still waiting to be found somewhere in the Valley of
the Kings.

Finding Tutankhamen's Tomb

Howard spent years searching the Valley of the Kings for Tutankhamen's tomb. Finally, he got
a lucky break. His team discovered some steps buried in the sand. As they dug deeper, they
uncovered a doorway that had Tutankhamen's name on it. Howard knew it had to be the tomb of
Tutankhamen.

Inside the Tomb

In ancient Egypt, pharaohs were buried with many **valuable objects**. When archaeologists
discovered the tomb of a pharaoh, they often found that robbers had already broken into the tomb
and emptied it. Howard hoped that Tutankhamen's tomb still held objects that would help him
learn more about ancient Egypt. What Howard found inside the tomb was beyond anything he
could have imagined.

There were four rooms inside the tomb, filled with objects. It turned out that robbers had broken into the tomb, but they had probably stolen only small objects that were easy to carry and sell. What the robbers had left behind was still a **treasure trove**. One of the most **spectacular** finds was a solid gold coffin that contained the **mummy** of Tutankhamen. There were so many objects inside the tomb that it took Howard and his team 10 years to clear out the tomb.

Emptying the Tomb

Why did it take so long to empty the tomb? There were four rooms inside the tomb (see the diagram). The tomb was emptied one room at a time. The **antechamber** alone contained over 700 objects.

Each object was **photographed** where it was found. Then a **sketch** was made of the object, along with a detailed description. After that, the location of the object was marked on a **map** of the tomb. Finally, the object was removed with great care.

Tutankhamen's tomb turned out to be one of the most amazing discoveries ever made in the Valley of the Kings.

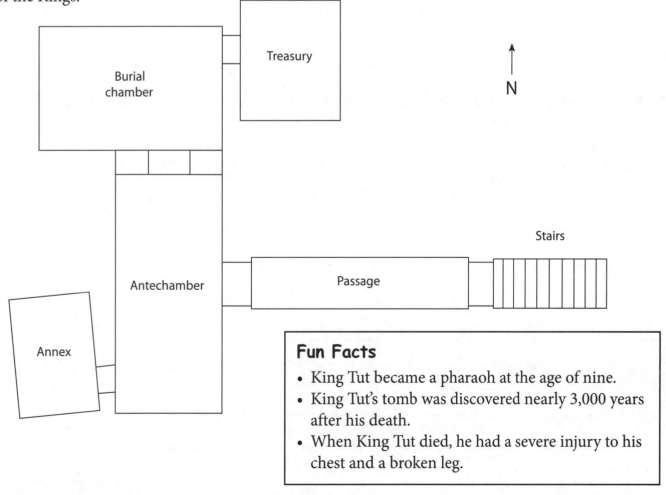

Fun Facts
- King Tut became a pharaoh at the age of nine.
- King Tut's tomb was discovered nearly 3,000 years after his death.
- When King Tut died, he had a severe injury to his chest and a broken leg.

"Discovering King Tut's Tomb"—Think About It

1. How did the Valley of the Kings get its name?

_____

_____

_____

2. Before Howard Carter discovered the tomb, what made him different from many archaeologists of his time?

_____

_____

_____

3. Use information in the text to help you write a definition of a "treasure trove."

_____

_____

_____

4. How was Howard's reason for entering the tomb different from the robbers' reason for entering the tomb?

_____

_____

_____

5. In what year did Howard and his team finish emptying the tomb? Tell how you know.

_____

_____

6. Why is Tutankhamen famous today?

_____

_____

_____

Discovering Exoplanets

What Is an Exoplanet?

An **exoplanet** is a planet that is **outside** our **solar system**. Planets in our solar system **orbit** around the star we call the Sun. Exoplanets also orbit around a **star**. Some of the stars you see in the night sky might have exoplanets orbiting around them.

Have Any Exoplanets Been Discovered?

Astronomers are people who study stars and other objects in space. For a long time, astronomers could only guess about whether some stars had exoplanets orbiting around them. The **technology** needed to find exoplanets did not yet exist. But technology improved over time, and astronomers discovered the first exoplanet in 1992. Since then, astronomers have discovered hundreds of exoplanets.

How Do Astronomers Discover Exoplanets?

Astronomers have two different ways of discovering exoplanets. The first way is called the **wobble method**. Like Earth and other planets, exoplanets have gravity that pulls on things around them. The Moon does not fly off into space because Earth's gravity pulls on it and keeps it close to Earth. Exoplanets also have gravity. An exoplanet's gravity pulls on the star it orbits around. This causes the star to wobble—to shift position a tiny bit. Exoplanets are too small and too far away for astronomers to see with telescopes. But when astronomers see a star wobble, they know there must be an exoplanet pulling on it.

The second way astronomers discover exoplanets is called the **transit method**. The word *transit* can mean "to pass across." Since an exoplanet orbits around a star, astronomers know that sometimes the exoplanet passes across the part of the star that they can see.

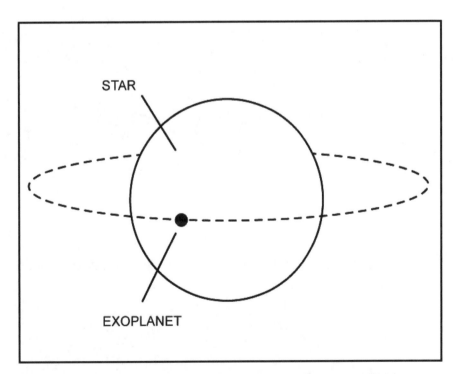

An exoplanet is passing across the part of a star that astronomers can see. The circle shows the path of the exoplanet's orbit.

If exoplanets are too small and too far away for astronomers to see, how can they tell if an exoplanet is passing across a star? Astronomers can record how much **light** is coming from a star. When an exoplanet passes across a star, it blocks some of the light coming from the star, so the star appears slightly **dimmer** for a time. When astronomers see that a tiny bit less light is coming from a star, they have a clue that an exoplanet might be passing in front of it.

Astronomers then keep watching star. If the star grows slightly dimmer over and over again, they know that there must be an exoplanet orbiting around the star.

Is There Life on Exoplanets?

Astronomers have not yet seen any evidence of life on exoplanets. They are now looking for planets that might have the right **conditions** for life. Astronomers know that an exoplanet that orbits very close to a star is probably far too hot for life to exist. If an exoplanet orbits too far from a star, it is probably too cold for life. Astronomers are looking for exoplanets that are not too close to or too far from a star. Finding an exoplanet like this does not guarantee that there will be some form of life on it, but it would be a good place to start looking.

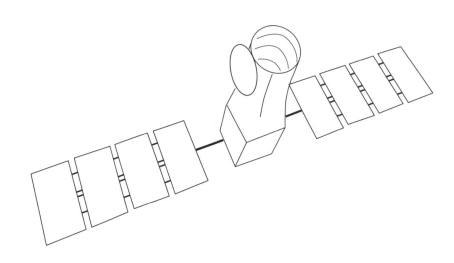

The COROT satellite's telescope uses the transit method to search for exoplanets.

"Discovering Exoplanets"—Think About It

1. The text mentions two ways that exoplanets are like the planets in our solar system. What are these two ways?

_____

_____

_____

2. What is one example of technology that astronomers use to search for exoplanets?

_____

_____

3. Why does an exoplanet cause a star to wobble?

_____

_____

4. Explain when and why an exoplanet makes a star look dimmer.

_____

_____

_____

5. If a star appeared a little bit dimmer just once, why would scientists know that the star did not get dimmer because an exoplanet was passing in front of it?

_____

_____

_____

6. Scientists believe that life could not exist on an exoplanet that does not have water. Why would there be no water on an exoplanet that orbits very close to a star?

_____

_____

_____

Who Rules Whom?

A **government** is the group of people (or person) who controls a **country**. A government makes **decisions** for the country. There are different **forms of government**. The way that a government controls and makes decisions is based on the form of government the country has. Let us look at two of these forms of government: a **democracy** and an **absolute monarchy**.

Democracy

Canada and the United States are both democracies. This means that the people **elect** their government. Every **citizen** over a certain age has the right to vote. Citizens can run for office, too. In a democracy, people have **freedom of speech**. So they can **criticize** the government if they do not like what it does.

Although both governments are democracies, they are not exactly the same. One difference is that in Canada, the queen or king of the United Kingdom is the **head of state**, and the **prime minister** is the **head of the governmen**t. (The head of state is the highest ranked position in a country.) In the United States, the **president** is the head of state as well as the head of the government.

Another difference is how the head of the government is elected. In Canada, the prime minister is the leader of the political party that gets the **most votes** in an election. In the United States, the president is elected **separately** from other people in the government.

Monarchy

In an absolute monarchy, a king or queen is the head of the government. He or she holds **all** the power. Many countries, such as France, Spain, and Russia, were absolute monarchies. Today, there are very few absolute monarchies. Two are Saudi Arabia and Swaziland in Africa.

Most monarchies today are **constitutional monarchies**. These governments still have queens or kings, but the kings or queens do **not have any real political power**. They are heads of state but not heads of the government. Some countries that are constitutional monarchies are Japan, Sweden, and Canada. So you can see that Canada is both a democracy and a constitutional monarchy.

"Who Rules Whom?"—Think About It

1. What does a government do? Use details from the text to support your answer.

_____

_____

2. What is the main idea of this text?

_____

_____

3. Complete the following graphic organizer to compare the governments of Canada and the United States.

Canada: Different	Same	United States: Different

4. What is the difference between an absolute monarchy and a constitutional monarchy?

_____

_____

5. The text says that a head of state is the highest ranked position in a country. What does this mean? Explain fully.

_____

_____

_____

What Does the President Do?

George Washington— the first president of the United States.

The United States is a big country with lots of people and many decisions to make. Americans elect a president to make those decisions.

Lawmaker

As the head of government for the United States, the president plays a large role in creating laws to make the United States a better place. However, the president cannot write laws himself/herself. To make laws, the president works with the members of Congress. Congress is made up of two groups of people who are elected by citizens across the United States to represent all Americans. One of these groups is called the Senate and the other group is the House of Representatives.

The president lets Congress know what new laws he/she thinks need to be passed and can also encourage them to pass these laws. When Congress wants to pass laws, the president can agree and pass them. The president can also disagree and veto, or reject, the laws. The president must also work with Congress to pass the federal budget, which says how the government will spend money.

Head of the Armed Forces

The president is Commander-in-Chief of the United States Armed Forces. This means he/she leads the Army, Navy, Air Force, Marine Corps, and Coast Guard, and is in charge of them. The president is the person who makes the final decision about what they will do. The United States has the largest armed forces of any country. That means the president is a very powerful person. The president must use his power carefully and responsibly.

What Else Does the President Do?

National, or federal, politicians belong to political parties. The parties are made up of people who think the same way about how to improve the country. Each party has a leader and the president of the United States is the leader of his political party.

National concerns that affect all Americans, such as the Post Office, immigration, and the environment, are also the president's responsibility. The president works with the Senate to appoint skilled people to be in charge of these different areas and to report to him/her.

The president also represents the United States at meetings with other countries around the world. He/she decides how his country will deal with other nations, negotiates agreements, or treaties, and appoints ambassadors to the other countries.

"What Does the President Do?"—Think About It

1. List three jobs the American president does. Use specific details from the text to support your answer.

_____

_____

_____

2. Name the two groups of people who help the president make laws.

_____

_____

3. Do you think Americans younger than 18 should be allowed to vote? Why or why not?

_____

_____

_____

4. What does the word veto mean? Use details from the text to support your answer.

_____

_____

_____

5. List two national issues that the president is responsible for.

_____

_____

6. Would you like to be president? Why or why not?

_____

_____

_____

Harriet Tubman

Harriet Tubman did not enjoy her life as a slave. She heard of a network of people who rescued slaves and led them to freedom. She decided to escape and help other slaves become free, too.

Born into Slavery
Harriet was an African American woman born around 1822 in Maryland. Her parents were slaves, which meant that Harriet was born a slave.

Like many slaves, Harriet was treated badly. Even when she was a little girl, she was whipped and beaten. She carried the scars for the rest of her life. One of her masters hit her on the head with a heavy weight. From then on, she suffered from severe headaches and seizures.

Escape!
Harriet could not stand being a slave any longer. On September 17, 1849, she escaped to Philadelphia where African Americans could be free. Then Harriet began thinking about her family members who were still enslaved. She was determined to rescue them. Harriet had to work slowly and carefully, but she eventually brought her relatives to freedom. Harriet then began helping others.

Moses
The slaves gave Harriet the nickname "Moses" after a man in the Bible who led people to freedom. Harriet became part of the Underground Railroad—the network of people who had helped her and many other African Americans escape from slavery.

This was not a real railroad, but it moved people around the country. The Underground Railroad helped escaped slaves in many ways, including giving them food, safe places to hide, and information about where they could go. The people helping groups of escaped slaves were called "conductors." Harriet was told a woman could not be a conductor, but she refused to accept this.

Conductors and Passengers
Harriet returned to the American south at least 19 times to help slaves escape. Thanks to Harriet's toughness and skill, not one of her passengers was ever caught. There was a $40,000 reward for her capture, but Harriet was never caught either. She freed about 300 slaves and was the Underground Railroad's most successful conductor.

"Harriet Tubman"—Think About It

1. What is the main idea of this text?

_____

_____

2. Harriet's nickname was "Moses." Why was this nickname given to her? Use details from the text to support your answer.

_____

_____

3. Read the text again, then write two other possible titles for it.

_____

_____

4. How many times did Harriet return to the American south?

_____

5. Why do you think they used the words "railroad," "conductor," and "passenger"?

_____

_____

6. Imagine you are an escaped slave just starting out on the Underground Railroad with Harriet. Write three sentences about how you feel and what you think of her.

_____

_____

_____

7. After reading about Harriet Tubman what do you wonder about?

_____

_____

Susan B. Anthony and Civil Rights

What Are Civil Rights?

Civil rights are the rights people have under the **laws** of the country they live in. In the United States, civil rights are protected by **The Constitution**. In Canada, civil rights are **protected** by the **Charter of Rights and Freedoms**. Every **citizen** in the United States or Canada has the **same** or **equal rights**. Some of these rights are the right to **free speech**, the right to a **fair trial**, and the right to **vote** in elections.

Susan B. Anthony and Her Fight for Equal Rights

Susan B. Anthony was born in Massachusetts in 1820. Her family believed in **education**, so she was sent to school. She was very **intelligent**. She could read and write by the time she was three.

Anthony's family also believed that men and women were **equal partners**. At that time, women in the United States did not have equal rights with men. In most states, married women could not own **property**. They could not keep the money they earned if they worked. Women were **paid** much less than men for the same work. They were not allowed to vote in elections.

Susan B. Anthony was a very **dedicated** woman. She fought for equal rights for everyone for most of her life. She is best known for her fight to get women the vote. She knew that the best way to get equal rights for women was to get them the vote. Then they could vote for people that could help them the most, and they could **run for office**, too.

Anthony began by giving **speeches** at meetings. She helped run a newspaper about civil rights. She even voted in an election even though it was against the law. She was put on **trial** for doing that. The **jury** at the trial was all men. Anthony was not allowed to speak. She was fined $100, which she never paid.

Then in 1869, she and Elizabeth Cady Stanton formed the **National Women's Suffrage Association**. (**Suffrage** means the right to vote.) Anthony worked with the organization until she died in 1906. She did not live to see her dream come true. The Constitution was changed in 1920 to give everyone the right to vote. Then no one could be refused the right to vote because of their **gender**.

"Susan B. Anthony and Civil Rights"—Think About It

1. What are civil rights? What examples of civil rights in the United States and in Canada are given in the text?

_____

_____

_____

2. The author says that Susan B. Anthony was a dedicated woman. What reasons does the author give for saying this?

_____

_____

_____

_____

3. What did Susan B. Anthony do to help women get the vote?

_____

_____

_____

4. What do you think the word _gender_ means? How do you know?

_____

_____

_____

5. How did getting the vote help women gain equal rights?

_____

_____

_____

6. When was the National Women's Suffrage Association formed?

Mark Twain

Many people call Mark Twain the first truly American writer. He wrote funny stories, but he also helped change the world by writing about human rights and racism.

Life on the Mississippi River

Mark Twain was born Samuel Langhorne Clemens in 1835 in Florida, Missouri. Sam loved watching the paddle-wheel steamboats move up and down the Mississippi River near his home. He even trained to be a steamboat pilot.

Famous Writer

As a young man, Sam had different jobs but he always kept writing. He even chose the pen name "Mark Twain." Where did that name come from? It is a steamboat term! Mississippi steamboats could travel safely when the river was at least two fathoms, or about 12 ft. (3.7 m) deep. That depth was called "mark twain." *Mark* referred to each 6-foot (1.8-m) mark on the rope used to measure the water depth, and *twain* is an old word meaning "two." So *mark twain* means "two marks."

Mark wrote many funny stories and newspaper articles. Soon Mark was writing books. They were instant bestsellers and Mark was very popular.

Tom and Huck

One of Mark's most famous books is *The Adventures of Tom Sawyer*, which was first published in 1876. Mark based the lead character, Tom, on himself and the story on his life in Hannibal, Missouri.

In 1885, Mark wrote *Adventures of Huckleberry Finn* about Tom's best friend Huck Finn. Huck told the story in his own words, using a lot of slang, and speaking the way real people spoke at the time. He even made grammar mistakes. It was the first book ever written that way, and was a new and very different way to tell a story. Mark's ideas changed books and literature forever.

Writer for Human Rights

Huck traveled with Jim, a runaway African American slave. Huck realized that Jim was a person, not an object someone could own.

Mark wanted to use his writing to make everyone see that racism is wrong. Mark's books still make people think about human rights, and help people understand how important freedom is for everyone.

"Mark Twain"—Think About It

1. Why did Samuel Clemens chose the name "Mark Twain"? Use details from the text to support your answer.

_____

_____

2. Why did Mark Twain write about racism? Use the text to support your answer.

_____

_____

_____

3. Besides writing, what other career was Sam interested in? Use the text to support your answer.

_____

_____

4. Why do you think Mark Twain based Tom Sawyer on himself and his own life?

_____

_____

5. In what ways was *Adventures of Huckleberry Finn* different from other books?

_____

_____

_____

6. List three types of texts that Mark wrote. Use the text to support your answer.

_____

_____

7. Why do you think Mark's books were popular? Use the text to support your answer.

_____

_____

A Gift from Wali Dad

(A traditional tale from India)

There was once a man named Wali Dad, who made his living as a **carpenter**. Wali Dad was happy living a very **simple life, buying** only the few things he needed. The rest of his money he put in a jar.

One day, Wali Dad noticed that the jar was full of coins. "I have nothing else to put money in," thought Wali Dad. "I must empty the jar." He took the jar to a jeweler and said, "Count this money, then sell me a bracelet worth the same amount." The jeweler sold Wali Dad a small gold bracelet. Wali Dad was pleased, but he had no idea what to do with the bracelet.

As he was going home, Wali Dad saw a **merchant** leading a camel loaded up with goods. "Where are you going?" asked Wali Dad.

"I am going to the palace," said the merchant. "I am delivering new clothes to the princess."

Wali Dad handed the merchant the bracelet. "Please give this to the princess," he said. "Tell her it is a gift from Wali Dad."

The princess thought the bracelet was a lovely gift. To thank him, she sent Wali Dad a camel loaded with fine **silk**.

The next day, Wali Dad saw the merchant standing outside his door. "I have brought you fine silk from the princess," said the merchant.

"Oh dear," said Wali Dad as he looked at the large load of silk. "I have no need of fine silk, and nowhere to put it in my tiny house. What will I do?"

"Send it to the **sultan**," said the merchant. "It is never a bad idea to send a gift to such a powerful person."

Wali Dad agreed. The merchant took the silk to the sultan, who was so pleased that in return he sent Wali Dad four strong horses. Wali Dad had no place to keep the horses, so he sent them to the princess.

"I do not know this person called Wali Dad," the princess said to her mother. "Why does he send me gifts?"

"He is trying to **impress** you with his **wealth**," said her mother. "This Wali Dad is too proud. Send him a gift that will show him how much wealthier you are. Perhaps then he will not be so proud."

The princess sent Wali Dad five camels loaded with silver. "This is much worse than a jar that is too full of coins!" moaned Wali Dad. He sent the silver to the sultan.

The sultan was certain that Wali Dad was trying to impress him by showing off his wealth. "I will send him six chests full of jewels. When he sees how wealthy I am, perhaps he will not be so proud."

When Wali Dad received the jewels, he sent them to the princess. "I must meet this man who sends me so many fine gifts," thought the princess. Accompanied by her maid, she set off to meet Wali Dad.

Just as she arrived at Wali Dad's house, the sultan appeared. He, too, had come to meet the man who sent such fine gifts. The princess and the sultan fell in love at first sight. Before long, they were married.

The sultan and the princess wanted to thank Wali Dad for bringing them together. They sent Wali Dad a very generous gift.

Wali Dad was just stepping out his door to go to work. He saw a man leading a horse pulling a cart. On the cart was a large chest. "This is your lucky day," the man told Wali Dad. "The sultan and his new wife have sent you this chest full of gold!"

"Oh, my!" said Wali Dad. "Could you just wait here a moment, please?" Wali Dad went into his house and ran out the back door. He was never seen again.

"A Gift from Wali Dad"—Think About It

1. What clue tells you that this story takes place a time long ago?

_____

_____

2. If Wali Dad had no use for a gold bracelet, why did he not sell it?

_____

_____

_____

3. Did Wali Dad send the silk to the sultan because he hoped the sultan would send him a better gift in return? Give a reason to support your answer.

_____

_____

_____

4. Why did the princess's mother and the Sultan think Wali Dad was proud?

_____

_____

_____

5. In what way did Wali Dad bring the sultan and the princess together?

_____

_____

_____

6. At the end of the story, why did Wali Dad run away and never come back?

_____

_____

_____

The Wise Judge

(A traditional tale from China)

Long ago in China, there was a judge who was **famous** throughout the land. When two people had a **dispute**, the judge was always able to find a **solution** that was **fair** to both people, whether they were rich or poor.

One day, the judge went to a busy market. **Merchants** were selling live chickens, fruits, vegetables, and just about anything else you could think of. As he walked through the market, the judge saw that a large crowd had gathered outside a shop that sold live chickens. The judge approached the crowd and asked a woman what was going on.

"A poor farmer was carrying a heavy sack," said the woman. "He accidentally tripped and dropped the sack on a chicken, killing it. The chicken belonged to the rich and greedy merchant who owns this shop," she said, pointing to the shop.

The judge could hear two men shouting at each other. "It was lucky I was passing by," thought the judge. "There is clearly a dispute going on, and I am going to solve it."

"Excuse me!" said the judge in a loud voice to the crowd. "Please let me through." When people turned and saw the judge, they quickly moved aside to let him pass through.

The two men who were arguing saw the judge approaching. They stopped yelling and bowed to the judge. "Please help us settle our dispute," they said.

The Wise Judge (continued)

"Tell me what happened," the judge said to the merchant who owned the shop that sold chickens.

"This farmer killed one of my chickens," said the merchant. "Now he must pay for it!"

The judge asked to see the dead chicken. "It is a quite a small young chicken," said the judge.

"That is true," said the merchant. "But in another two years that chicken would have grown large and plump. I can get 100 coins for a large, plump chicken. This farmer owes me 100 coins!"

The farmer was too terrified to speak. A hundred coins was a huge amount of money for him. Everyone in the town, including the judge, knew the farmer barely made enough money to buy clothes for his many children.

"I order you to pay this merchant 100 coins," the judge said to the farmer. The crowd gasped in shock. How could the farmer ever pay? The greedy merchant was overjoyed.

The judge turned to the merchant. "How much grain does a chicken eat in two years?" asked the judge.

"One large sack of grain," said the merchant. He exaggerated to justify the high prices he charged for his chickens.

"By killing this chicken, the farmer has saved you a large sack of grain," said the judge. "I order you to give the sack of grain you have saved to the farmer."

The merchant turned pale and hung his head. A large sack of grain was worth much more than 100 coins.

"I forgive this man for killing my chicken," said the merchant. "I will take no money from him, as long as I do not have to give him a sack of grain."

"As you wish," said the judge, who was seen to smile as he walked away.

"The Wise Judge"—Think About It

1. Use clues from the story to explain what a *dispute* is.

_____

_____

_____

2. Identify two events in the story that show people had great respect for the judge.

_____

_____

_____

3. Why did the merchant think that the small chicken was worth 100 coins?

_____

_____

_____

4. Why would the crowd be shocked when the judge ordered the farmer to pay the merchant 100 coins?

_____

_____

_____

5. Why did the judge smile when he walked away at the end of the story?

_____

_____

_____

6. In this story, did the judge live up to his reputation for being fair? Explain your opinion.

_____

_____

King of the World
(A traditional tale from Africa)

Long ago in Africa, there was a king who was **feared** by all his subjects. The king gave harsh **punishments** to anyone who did not show him the proper **respect**.

One day, the king went out among his people. A huge crowd gathered around the king, bowing and shouting out praise for him. "It is always so **delightful** to see how **powerful** I am," thought the king. "I treat my people **poorly**, yet look at how they praise me. Imagine how they would praise me if I were even more powerful!"

This gave the king an idea. He raised his hand to call for silence. Everyone stopped talking. They knew that anyone who spoke after the king had called for silence might be put to death.

"Today, I declare myself King of the World," the king announced. "All people in the entire world are my **servants**!"

The people were shocked. How could this man believe that every living person on the **planet** was his servant? But what happened next shocked the crowd even more.

"That is not true," said a voice from the crowd. "All people are servants of one another."

The king could not believe his ears. "Who dares to **disagree** with me?" he roared. "Let this man step forward."

An old man dressed in rags and carrying a walking stick came forward. People pushed and shoved to get a look at the man who was **foolish** enough to disagree with the king. Some people recognized the man. He traveled from village to village, doing odd jobs for people in exchange for a few bites of food.

Fury grew in the king's eyes as he stared at the old man. Finally, the king spoke. "Do you dare to suggest that I, the King of the World, am also a servant?" he thundered.

"We are all servants of each other," said the old man **humbly**.

"Then prove it to me by making me act as your servant," said the king. "You have until nightfall. If you fail, you will die. If you succeed, you will get a rich reward."

"I accept the **challenge**," said the old man. "Where I come from, we have a **custom**. When we accept a challenge from someone, we touch the person's feet. Hold my walking stick so I can honor you by touching your feet."

The king took the walking stick, and the old man knelt to touch the king's feet.

"Now give back my walking stick, so I can use it to stand up," said the old man. The king handed back the walking stick.

"I have given you the proof you asked for," said the old man.

The king was confused. "What **proof**?" he asked.

"A servant does as he is told," said the old man. "I told you to hold my walking stick, and you did. I told you to give back my walking stick, and you did. You have acted as my servant."

"You are both wise and very brave," said the king, who was impressed. "I will employ you as an **adviser**, and you will be well paid for your services."

"King of the World"—Think About It

1. Why would the king's subjects praise him if he treated them poorly?

_____

_____

_____

2. Why did the king declare himself King of the World?

_____

_____

_____

3. What do we mean when we say that someone "could not believe his ears"?

_____

_____

_____

4. Why could the king not believe his ears when the old man spoke up?

_____

_____

_____

5. How did the old man show that he was wise?

_____

_____

_____

6. Why would the king decide to employ the old man as an adviser, rather than just giving him money as a reward?

_____

_____

_____

The Teacher and the Thief

(A traditional tale from Japan)

There was once a great **teacher** named Benzei. Children from far and wide came to **study** at Benzei's school. Benzei loved his students and promised to do everything possible to help each one of them learn.

One day, a new student named Taku came to the school. Shortly after that, things started to go missing. The other students **suspected** that Taku was **stealing**. They decided to watch him and see if he really was the thief.

Before long, the students caught Taku stealing a pen. They went to Benzei and told him what they had seen. Everyone expected that Benzei would **expel** Taku from the school. Benzei did nothing. Taku continued to come to school each day.

Soon, Taku was caught stealing again. The students went to Benzei. Still Benzei did nothing. Word of the thief at Benzei's school soon spread throughout the village.

"What is wrong with Benzei?" asked one parent. "How can he allow a thief to stay at the school?"

"He does not **punish the thief** for stealing," said another parent. "He is setting a **bad example** for our children. They should learn that if they steal, they should expect to be punished."

"Benzei is now an old man," said the village doctor. "Perhaps his mind is starting to go. We must keep an eye on him and see if he is still fit to teach the children."

One man spoke up to defend Benzei. "Benzei was my teacher when I was a child, and I still visit him once a week. I can assure you that Benzei's mind is as strong as ever. There must be a reason why he does not punish the thief. Let us wait and see."

Once again, Taku was caught stealing. One of the students drew up a **petition** saying that if Taku was not expelled from the school, all the students who signed the petition would leave and go to another school. Every student except Taku signed the petition. Everyone was sure that now, finally, Taku would be expelled from the school.

Two of the older students presented the petition to Benzei. Benzei asked all the students in the school to gather together.

"I am proud of the students who signed this petition," said Benzei. "I can see that you have learned your lessons well, and you know right from wrong. Any school would be glad to accept you. But what about the student who has not learned right from wrong? What school would keep him for long? If I do not teach him, no one will. That is why I have not asked him to leave. I want all my students to learn."

Taku burst into tears when he realized how much Benzei cared about him. Taku never stole again.

None of the other students left Benzei's school. They knew that they would never find a teacher who cared more for his students than Benzei.

"The Teacher and the Thief"—Think About It

1. The beginning of the story tells a promise that Benzei made to his students. Does Benzei keep his promise? Provide support for your answer.

_____

_____

_____

2. Why did the students suspect that Taku was the person who was stealing?

_____

_____

3. What happens when a student is expelled from a school?

_____

_____

4. Before Benzei gathers all the students together, the story gives a clue that he has a reason for not expelling Taku. What is the clue?

_____

_____

_____

5. Why did the students believe that they would never find another teacher who would care more about them than Benzei?

_____

_____

_____

6. Benzei did not want to expel Taku. How else could Benzei have tried to deal with the problem of Taku's stealing?

_____

_____

A Great All-American Bird

They soar high in the sky, strong and powerful. The bald eagle is one of the largest birds in North America—and one of the most amazing too!

Not-So-Bald Bird

A bald eagle has mostly brown feathers. But its head has white feathers. So how did it become known as a bald eagle? The name "bald" comes from an old English word that means "white." Bald eagles also have white feathers on their tails and wing tips.

Skilled Hunter

Like most Eagles, the bald eagle is a bird of prey. That means it hunts other animals, such as birds, fish, snakes, and rabbits, to eat. With its large yellow eyes, a bald eagle can easily spot animals from a great distance. It can see a rabbit from as much as a mile (kilometer) away.

A bald eagle's sharp claws, or talons, can grab and hold on to any animal it catches. The bald eagle's long, curved, yellow beak allows it to devour its prey quickly.

Bald eagles can soar through the air for hours. When they dive while hunting, they can plummet at speeds of 100 mph (161 kph). That is as fast as a racecar drives!

Huge Nest

Bald eagles can be found across North America from Florida to Alaska. They live in forests near the shores of lakes and rivers.

High in a tree, a bald eagle builds a huge nest of twigs. The nest is called an aerie and can be as large as 8 ft. (2.4 m) across and weigh as much as a ton (tonne)! No bird in North America builds a bigger nest. An eagle might use the same nest year after year, repairing it and adding to it, which is how its nest becomes so large.

Proud Symbol

Since 1782, the bald eagle has been the national symbol of the United States. This beautiful bird appears on the presidential flag, the presidential seal, and other official seals of the American government. You can also see it on many coins and stamps.

"A Great All-American Bird"—Think About It

1. What is the main idea of the sections titled "Skilled Hunter" and "Huge Nest"?

_____

_____

_____

2. Explain how the bald eagle got its name. Use specific details from the text to support your answer.

_____

_____

_____

3. Where can you find pictures of the bald eagle in the United States? Write the sentences from the text you used to get this answer.

_____

_____

_____

_____

4. The bald eagle is described as a national symbol. What do you think this means?

_____

_____

_____

5. What is the name given to an eagle's nest?

_____

6. What are three interesting facts you learned about bald eagles by reading this text?

_____

_____

_____

Graphic Organizers

Graphic organizers are excellent tools to use for identifying and organizing information from a text into an easy-to-understand visual format. Students will expand their comprehension of a text as they complete the graphic organizers. Use these graphic organizers in addition to the activities in this book or with other texts.

Concept Web – Helps students understand the main idea of a text and how it is supported by key details.

Concept Map – Helps students gain a better understanding of how different subtopics within a text connect to the topic as a whole.

Venn Diagram/Comparison Chart – Helps students focus on the comparison of two items, such as individuals, ideas, events, or pieces of information. Students could compare by looking at which things are the same, or contrast by looking at which things are different.

Fact or Opinion – Helps students to distinguish between statements of fact or opinion. Facts are pieces of information that can be proven to be true. Opinions are pieces of information based on something that someone thinks or believes, but that cannot necessarily be proven to be true.

Cause and Effect – Helps students to recognize and explain relationships between events. The cause is the reason why an event happens and the effect is the event that happens.

Making Connections – Helps students to connect something they have read, or experienced, with the world around them.

Context Clue Chart – Helps students organize clues that the author gives in a text to help define a difficult or unusual word. Encourage students to look for explanations of words within a text.

Drawing Conclusions and Making Inferences Chart – Helps students practice drawing conclusions and making inferences based on their prior knowledge, as well as what they read in the text.

A Concept Web About...

A **main idea** is what the text is mostly about. A **detail** is important information that tells more about the main idea.

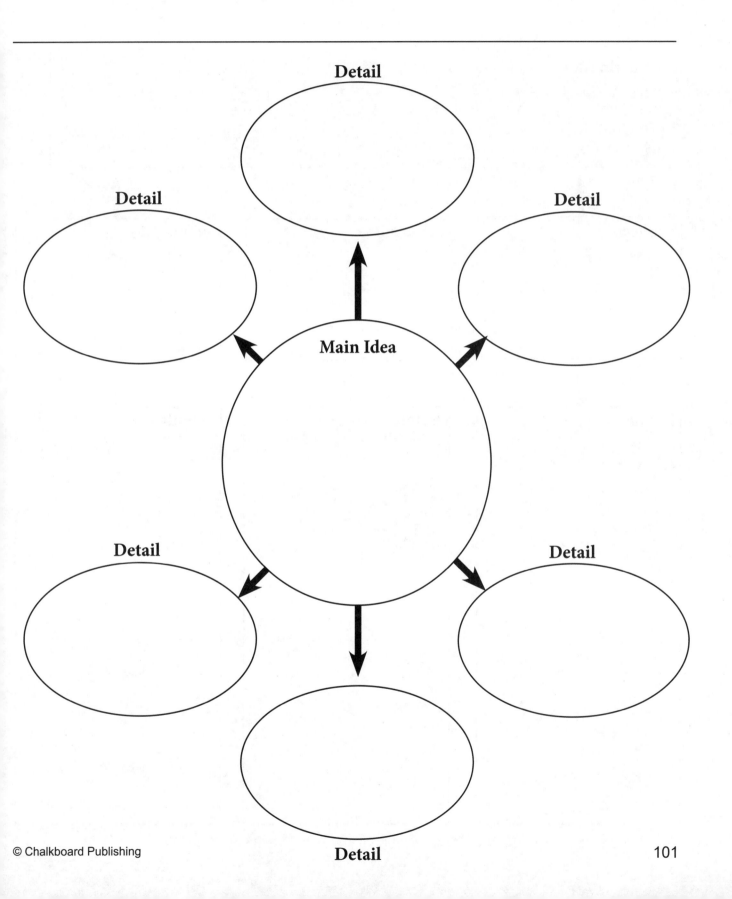

Detail

Detail

Detail

Main Idea

Detail

Detail

Detail

Concept Map

A **main idea** is what the text is mostly about.
A **subheading** is the title given to a part of a text.
A **detail** is important information that tells more about the main idea.

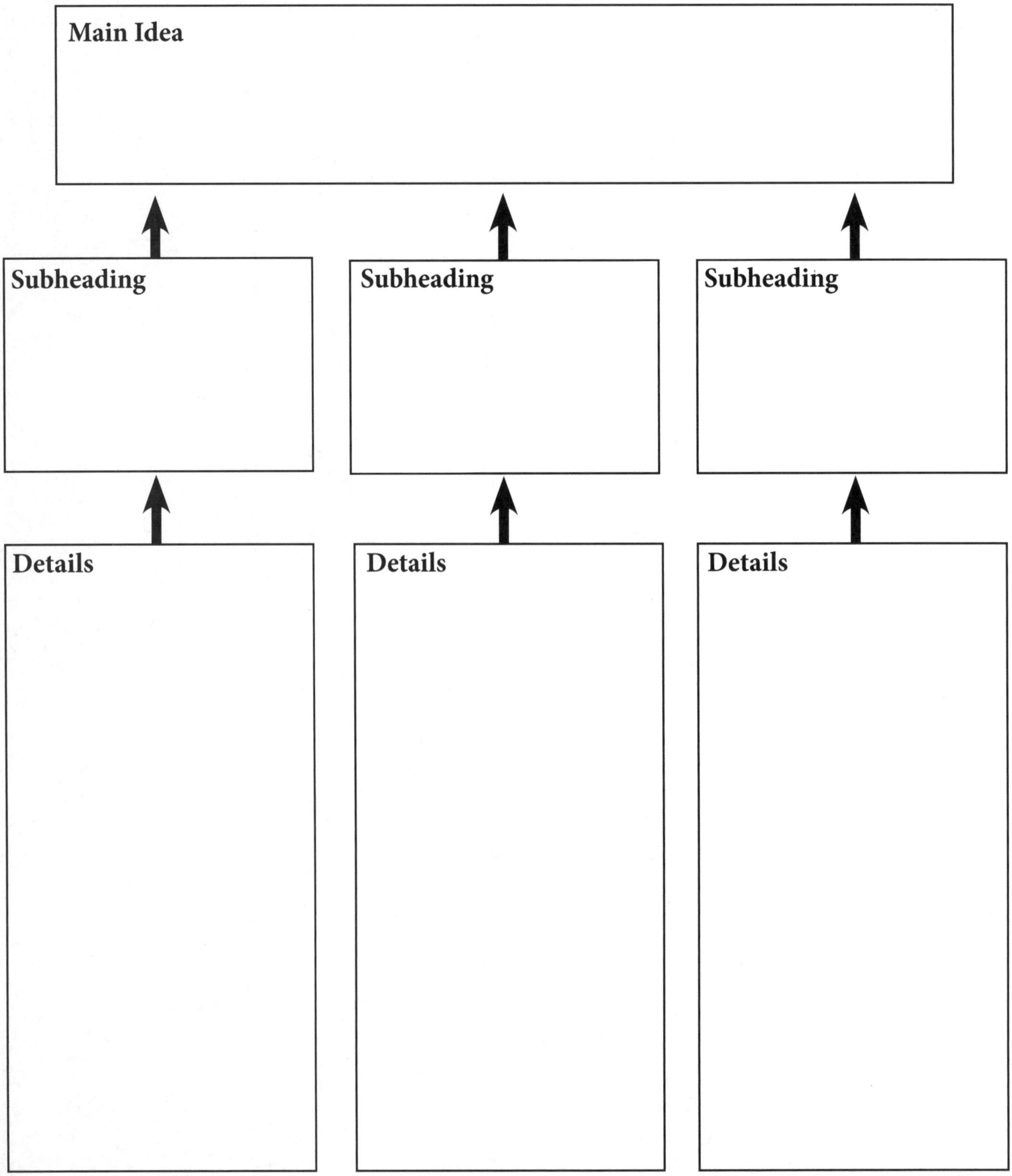

Main Idea

Subheading

Subheading

Subheading

Details

Details

Details

A Venn Diagram About...

_____

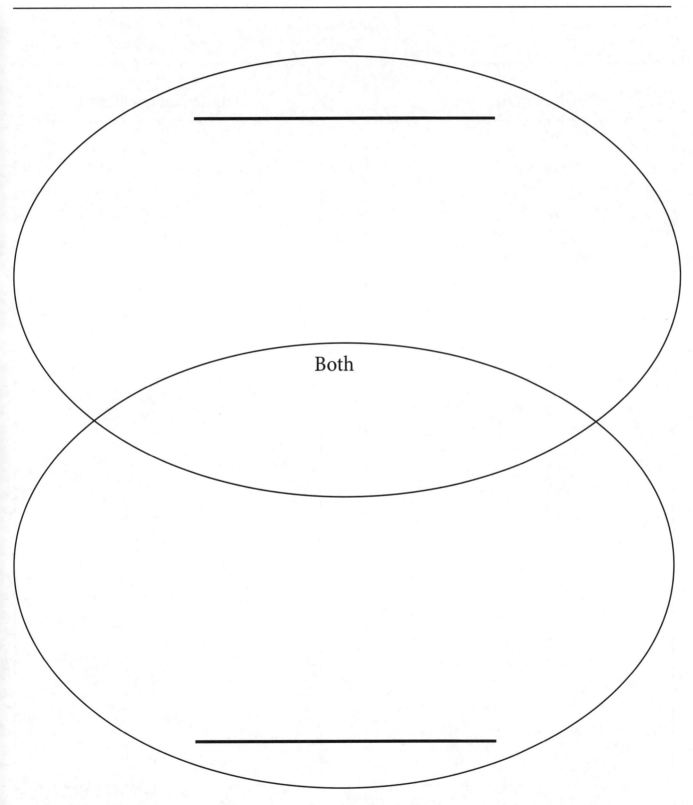

Both

A Comparison Chart

Compared
to

Detailed information

Detailed information

Fact or Opinion

- **Facts** are pieces of information that can be proven to be true.
- **Opinions** are pieces of information based on something a person thinks or believes.

Piece of Information	Fact or Opinion?	How do you know?

Cause and Effect

- The **cause** is the reason something happens.
- The **effect** is what happened.

Cause

Effect

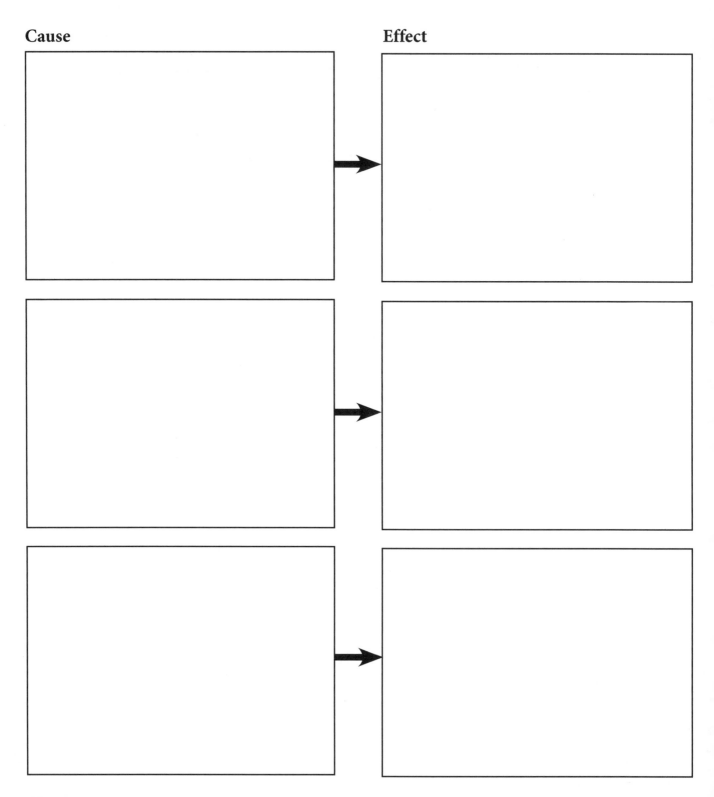

Making Connections with What I Have Read

After reading…	It reminds me of…	This helps me make a connection to…
		☐ something else I have read ☐ myself ☐ the world around me
		☐ something else I have read ☐ myself ☐ the world around me
		☐ something else I have read ☐ myself ☐ the world around me
		☐ something else I have read ☐ myself ☐ the world around me

Context Clue Chart

Context Clues are hints that the author gives in a text that can help you find the meaning of a word.

Word	Context Clue from Text	Meaning of Word

108

Drawing Conclusions and Making Inferences Chart

We make an **inference** when we combine what we know to be true with new information and come to a conclusion.

What I already know:

Clues from the text I read:

Help me to conclude or infer:

How Am I Doing?

	Completing my work	Using my time wisely	Following directions	Keeping organized
Full speed ahead!	• My work is always complete and done with care. • I added extra details to my work.	• I always get my work done on time.	• I always follow directions.	• My materials are always neatly organized. • I am always prepared and ready to learn.
Keep going!	• My work is complete and done with care. • I added extra details to my work.	• I usually get my work done on time.	• I usually follow directions without reminders.	• I usually can find my materials. • I am usually prepared and ready to learn.
Slow down!	• My work is complete. • I need to check my work.	• I sometimes get my work done on time.	• I sometimes need reminders to follow directions.	• I sometimes need time to find my materials. • I am sometimes prepared and ready to learn.
Stop!	• My work is not complete. • I need to check my work.	• I rarely get my work done on time.	• I need reminders to follow directions.	• I need to organize my materials. • I am rarely prepared and ready to learn.

Reading Comprehension Student Tracking Sheet

Student's Name	Identifies the Purpose of the Text *Student: I can tell you why we read this.*	Demonstrates Understanding of the Text *Student: I can tell you what the text is about.*	Analyzes Text *Student: I can make predictions, interpretations, and conclusions using information from the text.*	Makes Connections to Text (Prior Knowledge) *Student: This reminds me of* • *text-to-text* • *text-to-self* • *text-to-world*	Text Features *Student: I can tell you how different text features help the reader.*

Level 4: Student shows a thorough understanding of all or almost all concepts and consistently gives appropriate and complete explanations independently. No teacher support is needed.

Level 3: Student shows a good understanding of most concepts and usually gives complete or nearly complete explanations. Infrequent teacher support is needed.

Level 2: Student shows a satisfactory understanding of most concepts and sometimes gives appropriate, but incomplete explanations. Teacher support is sometimes needed.

Level 1: Student shows little understanding of concepts and rarely gives complete explanations. Intensive teacher support is needed.

You Are Doing Wonderful!

Keep Up the Excellent Work!

_____

Name

_____

Date

Reading Comprehension

Answers

Earthquakes, pp. 6–7

1. Huge slabs of rock under Earth's surface.
2. Students should complete the chart as follows

Cause	Effect
Two tectonic plates get stuck as they rub against each other.	Force builds up as the plates keep trying to move.
There is enough force to make the plates move again.	The plates move quickly for a few moments.
The plates move quickly for a few moments.	*This movement causes the surface of Earth to tremble and shake.*
An earthquake is so weak that people do not notice it.	*There is no damage.*
A powerful earthquake causes the ground to shake a lot.	There is a lot of damage to buildings and other structures.

3. People have put in place rules for building new structures strong enough to stand up to most earthquakes.
4. Many older structures were built before rules were put in place to make buildings strong enough to stand up to earthquakes.

Hurricanes, pp. 8–9

1. Question and answer. Each subheading is a question, and the text under each subheading answers the question.
2. First main idea: A hurricane is a huge storm that forms over warm ocean water. Second main idea: Strong winds and heavy rain can do a lot of damage when a hurricane moves over land.
3. Students should list two of the following pieces of evidence:
   • Hurricane winds can move at speeds from 75 mph (120 kph) to over 186 mph (300 kph).
   • Hurricane winds can be strong enough to shatter windows.
   • Hurricane winds can knock over tall trees.
   • Hurricane winds can pick up objects such as patio furniture and send them flying with great force into buildings.
   • Hurricane winds can make a storm surge move with enough force to move or destroy a house.
4. The eye and eye wall of the hurricane are passing over the city. The winds are much weaker in the eye of the storm.
5. The house might no longer be safe because floodwater makes the wood in the house weaker, so the house might collapse.

Tornado Alert! pp. 10–12

1. No. A tornado starts to form in a storm cloud, so a tornado could not form on a day when the sky is clear.
2. A funnel cloud is shaped like a funnel. Both are wider at the top than at the bottom.
3. No. Tornado A could have been traveling more slowly than Tornado B but lasted longer, so it left a longer path.
4. The cloud is also moving at 31 mph (50 kph). Every tornado moves along with the cloud above it.
5. Yes. Since tornado watches happen when the conditions are right for a tornado, weather experts must be able to tell when a tornado might form.
6. Students should record two of the following main ideas:
   • A tornado can be one of the most dangerous storms in nature.
   • A tornado does not stay in one place.
   • Weather reports tell people about tornado watches and tornado warnings.

Avalanches and Landslides, pp. 13–14

1. Comparison
2. A slope is a slanted surface.
3. Water gets between the particles of soil, reducing the friction between them, so gravity can pull the soil down.
4. The snow on top of the roof becomes so heavy that it cannot resist gravity, so gravity makes the snow slide down off the roof.
5. Possible similarities include:
   • Both involve material falling down a slope.
   • Both can happen on the side of a mountain or a tall hill.
   • Gravity pulls material down in both types of events.
   • Both are caused by precipitation.
   • Both are usually started by a trigger event (vibrations).
6. Possible differences include:
   • Snow falls in an avalanche, and soil falls in a landslide.
   • Avalanches happen when a lot of snow builds up on a slope. Landslides happen when soil on a slope gets wet.
7. A trigger event is something that makes the snow or soil unstable. Students should give one of the following examples from the text: vibrations from an earthquake, an erupting volcano, or a very loud sound are examples of trigger events.

Tsunami: Killer Waves, pp. 15–16

1. A tsunami is a series of huge waves of water caused by an earthquake under the sea or an erupting volcano.

2. The earthquake struck off the coast so the people nearby didn't have a lot of time to get to higher ground.
3. The waves push the objects along, smashing them into everything in their path.
4. Lots of people in vehicles would cause traffic jams so they would not be able to get away quickly or maybe not at all.
5. The map helps the reader know the location of the Tsunami.

Good Bones, pp. 17–18

1. My body would look like a puddle on the floor because there would not be anything to hold my body up. Everything would be a big jumble inside my skin.
2. Playing basketball or volleyball would be weight-bearing. Climbing stairs or running would be weight-bearing. These are weight-bearing because your feet leave the ground, then come back down. You are working against gravity when you do this.
3. As a baby grows, some of the bones grow together. So an adult would have fewer bones than a baby.
4. The text has an introduction, then three parts. The subheadings tell me what is going to be in each part so I have an idea about what I will be reading.
5. *Flexible* means to be able to bend easily. Babies' bones are softer and more flexible so they can move their bones in different ways. As they grow up and their bones get harder, they cannot do the same things.
6. Some baby bones are partly cartilage. Cartilage is softer than bone. That is why babies are so flexible. They can move their bones in ways that adults cannot.
7. Bones are alive because they can grow. Only living things can grow.

When a Bone Breaks, pp. 19–20

1. The author wants to explain that bones can bend a little, but that they will break if they bend too much.
2. A doctor takes an X-ray to find out if a bone is broken and to find out how to set a broken bone.
3. "Setting a bone" means moving the pieces of the broken bone back to their normal position.
4. a) A person with a broken bone has to wear a cast for one to two months.
   b) "It can take from one to two months for a broken bone to heal."
5.

Cause	Effect
A doctor sets the broken bone.	The pieces of broken bone are now back in their normal position.
A cast is put around the part of the body where the broken bone is.	*The broken pieces of bone do not move while they heal.*
The bone makes many new cells to heal the break.	The broken pieces of bone stick together and slowly make the bone as good as new.

Moving with Muscles, pp. 21–22

1. A muscle is getting shorter and thicker when it contracts.
2. A muscle is getting longer and thinner when it relaxes.
3. If one muscle in a pair is contracting, the other muscle is relaxing.
4. Your brain sends signals to the muscles you need to use to jump.
5. A voluntary muscle is a muscle you can control. An involuntary muscle is a muscle that you do not control.
6. These are involuntary muscles. The muscles work on their own. You do not need to think about moving the food down to your stomach.

Your Cardiovascular System, pp. 23–25

1. The heart, blood, and blood vessels all work together to move blood from the heart to all parts of the body, then back again.
2. Sample summary sentences:
   The Heart: Your heart beats to squeeze blood into blood vessels, then pull more blood into the heart.
   Blood: Blood is made of plasma, red blood cells, white blood cells, and platelets.
   Blood Vessels: Arteries, veins, and capillaries are three different types of blood vessels.
   Blood and Oxygen: Blood gets oxygen in the lungs then travels back to the heart, so the blood and oxygen can be pumped through all parts of the body.
3. Blood carries oxygen to all parts of the body, helps the body fight germs, and repairs the body after an injury.
4. A human hair is about 10 times thicker than most capillaries.
5. There are about 5 million red blood cells in one tiny drop of blood. I got the information from the Fun Facts box.

Are You Getting Enough ZZZs? pp. 26–27

1. I can eat good food, get a lot of exercise, and get enough sleep.
2. Blue light helps you stay awake during the day so you can do things you need to do.
3. Ten hours of sleep can help you stay awake and be more active during the day. You might not get sick. Your body will be healthier and might grow better.
4. We do not have a real 24-hour clock inside our bodies. The author used the idea because one day is 24 hours long. We are awake part of a day and asleep the other part. A clock tells us the hours when we should be awake and when we should be asleep.
5. Answers will vary. Some students might say that kids should have a regular bedtime because it is easier for their body to get used to going to sleep at the same time every night, and it would be healthier for them. Other students might say that kids should be allowed to stay up later on special occasions and maybe on weekends.

114 © Chalkboard Publishing

More Vitamin C, Please, pp. 28–29

1. Freshly squeezed orange juice had the most Vitamin C because its solution was the lightest color.
2. The instructions under "What You Do" are numbered because they need to be done in the right order. If you did not do them in the right order, the experiment might not work. Numbers are not used in What You Need because it is just a list of materials.
3. Indicator means something that shows or points out. Indicate is the verb and indicator is the noun of the same word. An indicator solution is a solution that shows something or points out something.
4. If you hold the test tubes against a white background, you will be able to see the colors of the solution better.
5.

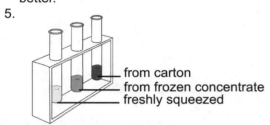

from carton
from frozen concentrate
freshly squeezed

Calories—We Need Them, pp. 30–33

1. Calories are a measurement. Calories tell you how much energy you can get from the food you eat and drink.
2. Fat protects organs such as the liver. It helps keep your body at the right temperature. It keeps your hair and skin healthy. It provides you with energy.
3. How many calories you need depends on your age and how active you are.
4. You need different foods in the right amounts to get the nutrients you need.
5. A food guide is a document created by the government health department. A food guide tells people what types of foods to eat, and how much to eat, to have a healthy body.
6. Too much fat can make you gain weight you do not need. The extra weight can cause health problems as you get older.
7. Boys need more calories than girls in every category.
8. Not very active means you spend most of your time sitting. Active means doing some things like walking and getting some exercise. Very active means getting a lot of exercise.
9. Answers will vary. Sample answers: Try to get most of your calories from healthy foods and limit the amount of junk food you eat. Check a food guide to find out how many calories you should have in a day and what types of foods you should be eating.
10. Ensure that students list three facts from the Fun Facts box.

Gluten and Lactose, pp. 34–35

1. A balanced diet will give you all the nutrients you need to grow and stay healthy.
2. It is describing two problems people can have if their digestive system does not work right. One problem is having celiac disease. The other is being lactose intolerant.
3. *Symptom* means something that happens to you if you get sick. People with celiac disease get stomachaches and diarrhea. The text says that these are symptoms of celiac disease.
4. *Lactose intolerant* means being unable to digest the sugar that is found in milk and dairy products.
5.

	Gluten (celiac disease)	Lactose (lactose intolerant)
Foods it is found in	foods that contain wheat, barley, or rye	*dairy products*
Part of digestive system affected	*small intestine*	small and large intestine
Symptoms	stomachaches, diarrhea, not wanting to eat, losing weight, not growing properly, skin rash	gas, pain or cramps, diarrhea, throwing up
Best way to treat	Do not eat foods that contain gluten	*Do not eat foods that contain lactose*

6. Students should list any three of the following: broccoli, kale, salmon, almonds, fortified orange juice, tofu.

Read That Label! pp. 36–37

1. Natural foods have nothing added to them before you cook them or eat them raw. Processed foots have other things added to them before you eat them.
2. a) The third ingredient is sugar/glucose-fructose. This tells me that sugar is the third-largest ingredient in the cereal.
   b) Sample answer: I would want to know exactly how much sugar is in the cereal.
3. All these words end in "ose." I think maltose is a sugar because it ends in "ose."
4. The main idea for "The Ingredient List" is that all processed foods have an ingredient list that tells you what is in the food. The main idea for "What's in a Name?" is that fat, sodium, and sugar can have different names in an ingredient list.
5. Salt is made from sodium. We need to be careful about how much salt we eat so we do not get too much sodium in our bodies.

Mysteries of Stonehenge, pp. 38–40

1. Possible answers include strong winds pushing on the rocks, erosion and weathering from rain and wind, shifting and cracking from freeze-thaw cycles.
2. a) An inclined plane may have been used as a ramp to pull the lintels up to the top of the standing stones.
   b) A lever might have been used to tip the standing stones into holes to make them stand securely.
3. Answers will vary.

The Hoover Dam, pp. 41–43

1. Answers will vary. Sample answers: Yes, I think building dams is a good idea because they provide a lot of jobs and can cheaply produce a lot of electricity that everyone needs. No, I do not think building dams is a good idea because the water floods animal habitats, kills a lot of plants and trees, and sometimes floods people's lands. Dams ruin the environment.
2. The Hoover Dam is used to provide hydroelectricity.
3. The name changed because they wanted to name it after Herbert Hoover, who was the American president at the time the dam was being built.
4. Answers will vary.
5. More than a million people visit the Hoover Dam each year.
6. Answers will vary. Ensure that students describe what impressed them about the building.
7. The Hoover Dam was completed on March 1, 1936.

Famous Bridges, pp. 44–45

1. Lake Pontchartrain Causeway has four lanes.
2. The suspension bridge is the newest. Arch bridges were built by the Romans. Beam bridges are older than arch bridges. Suspension bridges must be the newest because they use steel cables. The Romans did not have steel.
3.

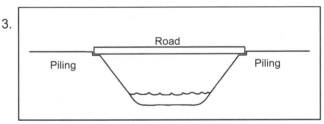

The horizontal beams are under the road. Vertical means something that goes up and down. Horizontal means something that goes across or from side to side.
4. In a suspension bridge, the road is held up or supported by smaller cables that are attached to the big cables. So the road is suspended from the bigger cables. *Suspension* and *suspended* have the same meaning but they are used differently in sentences.
5. It means that it connects two nations or countries. It connects the United States and Canada.

Why Igloos Work, pp. 46–47

1. In the summer the Inuit lived in huts made from animal skins. In the winter they lived in igloos made from snow.
2. Seals live in the sea and on ice. They can live where it is very cold.
3. The Inuit ate mostly meat because they lived in the tundra. There are very few plants in the tundra.
4. Sample answer: Igloos are made from snow. You do not need a lot of tools to make them. They are strong because they are shaped like a dome. Igloos stop the wind from getting inside. The snow and ice act like an insulator so it is warmer inside. They can be any size.
5. Insulator means something that keeps heat in. The text says that snow is a good insulator and it keeps heat inside the igloo.
6. The author gives the information in points. This helps me because I know that all the information in each point will be about one main idea.

How Buildings Kill Birds, pp. 48–49

1. Sample summaries:
   • First paragraph: Birds fly into windows because they are trying to get to plants they see inside buildings.
   • Second paragraph: Birds try to fly into the reflections they see on buildings that have mirrored glass.
2. Birds that migrate at night use the moon and stars to guide them in the right direction.
3. The bird's instinct is to fly toward light, but it will fly into glass when it flies toward light inside a window.
4. Dead birds are removed from the bottom of office buildings long before people start arriving for work, so people do not see any dead birds.
5. Turning off the lights means fewer birds fly into buildings, and the building uses less energy for lighting.

How Does That Fly? pp. 50–51

1. Gravity wants to pull the plane down to Earth. Drag wants to pull the plane backward. Lift and thrust overcome these two forces so a plane can fly.
2. The diagram relates to the part on weight, lift, drag, and thrust. It helped me understand the information better because it shows which forces act against each other and the direction the forces act in. It summarizes what the writing says.
3. When an airplane is flying straight and level, weight is equal to lift, and drag is equal to thrust.
4. It means to use the smallest amount of fuel to get somewhere. Fuels that are efficient will get a plane farther than fuels that are not as efficient.
5. Jet engines are more powerful so the planes can fly faster. The faster they fly, the more lift they have. So planes can be bigger and still fly.
6. Airplanes today can carry more passengers because they are much bigger. Airplanes today can fly farther. Airplanes today have jet engines

Fill It Up! pp. 52–53

1. Gasoline is the most common fuel for vehicles. Crude oil is refined to make gasoline for vehicles.
2. Crude oil is also called petroleum. Crude oil contains different types of hydrocarbons.
3. Vehicles can run on gasoline, ethanol, biodiesel, compressed natural gas, electricity, or a combination of electricity and another fuel.
4. Sample answer:

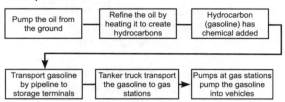

5. *Compressed* means to squeeze something to make it smaller. The text says that compressed natural gas is squeezed so it takes up less space.

Geothermal Electricity, pp. 54–57

1. *Generated* means "created" or "made."
2. For each main idea, students should record two of the supporting details below:

Main idea: Most electricity is generated at power plants.
• Spinning magnets inside a generator create electricity.
• The magnets spin because they are connected to a turbine that spins.
• It takes energy to make the turbine spin.

Main idea: There are different ways to make a turbine spin.
• Some power plants use the energy of moving water, such as a waterfall, to make a turbine spin.
• Steam can make a turbine spin.
• Coal and oil can be burned to create steam to spin a turbine.

3. The energy of moving water can be used to make a turbine spin. There is a lot of moving water in a waterfall.
4. The pipe is called the injection well. This pipe is labeled in the diagram.
5. Geothermal power plants do not pollute the air by burning coal or oil to change water to steam. The hot underground water that geothermal power plants use is a renewable resource.
6. Answers will vary.

Power from the Wind, pp. 58–61

1. Leon's point of view is that wind turbines are "great" and an "excellent alternative." Kerry's point of view is that wind turbines are "a pretty good way to produce energy," but they are not perfect.
2. Leon and Kerry both make the following points to support the idea of wind turbines:
   • Wind turbines do not use up fossil fuels.
   • Wind turbines do not create pollution.

3. Students should record the following benefits:

Benefit	Writer
Wind turbines do not contribute to climate change.	Leon
Wind turbines are cheaper to build than power-generating plants.	Kerry

4. Kerry does not offer a solution to the problem of wind turbines killing birds.
5. Responses may vary. Many students might feel that Kerry's text would be most likely to persuade readers because it addresses some of the problems of wind turbines.
6. Answers will vary.

When Water Changes State, pp. 62–63

1. The solution froze because it had water in it. The water froze when the temperature got colder.
2. Salt is put on black ice because it lowers the freezing temperature of ice and can change the ice back into water.
3. Water will evaporate at any temperature. It will evaporate faster when the temperature is higher and slower when the temperature is lower.
4. A subheading could be placed before the first paragraph about black ice (Changes in the state of matter...) and before the first paragraph on evaporation (Problems can also happen...). The first subheading could be about black ice or water freezing. The second subheading could be about losing water from reservoirs or water evaporating.
5. a) *Transparent* means clear and easy to see through. The text says that black ice should be called "clear ice." It says that you can see the road through the ice. b) Glass is transparent.
6. Reservoirs store large amounts of water. Water will evaporate. Reservoirs lose a lot of water through evaporation.

What Is a Landfill? pp. 64–66

1. Students should record two of the following details:
   • A city produces large amounts of garbage year after year.
   • Most landfills cover a lot of land so they can hold a lot of garbage.
   • Once a landfill can hold no more garbage, a new landfill must be created.
   • A community might need empty land for building new houses or factories, or for farmland.
2. Students should suggest definitions similar to the following examples:
   • A barrier is something that stops things from moving past a certain point.
   • A barrier prevents things from going any farther.
   • A barrier keeps two things apart.

3. Students should offer the following reasons:
   - Leachate can contain dangerous chemicals from the landfill.
   - Leachate can pollute soil and underground water.
   - Dangerous chemicals in leachate might end up in drinking water.
4. If any leachate leaks through the plastic liner, the leachate is absorbed by the clay. The clay keeps the leachate from seeping into the soil under the landfill.
5. The landfill could become a park or a sports field that people in the community can use.
6. When people recycle, less garbage goes into landfills.

The Dinofish, pp. 67–69
1. Sample answers:
   - Scientists thought that the coelacanth had become extinct at the same time that dinosaurs became extinct.
   - Coelacanths were living at the same time dinosaurs were alive.
2. The overall structure is chronology. The text tells a series of events in the order that they happened.
3. Two reasons why Marjorie almost did not discover the coelacanth:
   - She almost did not go to the docks on December 3 because she was busy at the museum.
   - She did not go to the docks to look at the fish that had been caught. She was just about to leave when she noticed a strange fin.
4. Marjorie compared the fish to pictures in books, and she sent a drawing of the fish to a fish expert.
5. The only way to know that coelacanths appear to stand on their head is to observe live coelacanths in the ocean.
6. Answers will vary.

Discovering King Tut's Tomb, pp. 70–72
1. Many pharaohs were buried there, and pharaohs were like kings in ancient Egypt.
2. Howard believed that Tutankhamen's tomb was in the Valley of the Kings. Most other archaeologists at the time believed that there were no more tombs to be found in the Valley of the Kings.
3. A treasure trove is a large collection of valuable objects.
4. Howard wanted to enter the tomb to find objects that would help him learn more about ancient Egypt. Robbers wanted to enter the tomb to find valuable objects that they can sell.
5. Howard and his team finished emptying the tomb in 1932. The text says that the tomb was discovered in 1922, and it took 10 years to empty the tomb.
6. Tutankhamen is famous today because his tomb was one of the most amazing discoveries ever made in the Valley of the Kings.

Discovering Exoplanets, pp. 73–75
1. Exoplanets and the planets in our solar system all orbit around a star, and they all have gravity.
2. The COROT space telescope is one example of technology that astronomers use to search for exoplanets.
3. The gravity of an exoplanet pulls on the star it orbits around, causing it to wobble.
4. An exoplanet makes a star look dimmer when it passes in front of the part of the star that astronomers can see. The star looks dimmer because the exoplanet blocks some of the light coming from the star.
5. An exoplanet would orbit around and around a star, so it would make the star look dimmer over and over again.
6. An exoplanet that orbits very close to a star would be so hot that any water on it would evaporate.

Who Rules Whom? pp. 76–77
1. A government controls a country and makes decisions for it.
2. There are different forms of government. Democracies and monarchies are two forms.
3.

Canada: Different	Same	United States: Different
- king or queen of United Kingdom is head of state - prime minister is head of government - prime minister is head of political party that gets the most votes in an election - Canada is also a constitutional monarchy	- both are democracies - citizens can vote for their government - citizens can run for office - people have freedom of speech	- president is head of state and head of government - president is elected separately from other people in the government

4. In an absolute monarchy, the king or queen has all the power. The absolute monarch is the head of state as well as the head of the government. In a constitutional monarchy, the king or queen does not have any real political power. He or she is only the head of state.
5. There is no one in the country that has a higher position. A head of state is at the top of everyone. It is like being a principal in a school. The principal is the highest position in a school. The head of state may have a lot of power, or may not have much power. It depends on the form of government.

What Does the President Do? pp. 78–79

1. The president's jobs include making laws and rules with the help of Congress, being head of his political party, creating a federal budget, representing the United States to other countries, appointing ambassadors, being responsible for federal organizations such as the Post Office, and being Commander-in-Chief of the United States Armed Forces.
2. The two groups that help the president make laws are the Senate and the House of Representatives.
3. Answers will vary. Sample answers: Yes, I think Americans younger than 18 should be allowed to vote because young people need to have a voice, too. No, I do not think Americans younger than 18 should be allowed to vote because most young people might not know enough about politics to make the right choice.
4. The word veto means to reject a proposed bill. The text says the president can "veto or reject the laws."
5. Students should choose two of the following national issues that the president is responsible for: the Post Office, immigration, and the environment.
6. Answers will vary.

Harriet Tubman, pp. 80–81

1. The main idea of this text is that Harriet Tubman was an important person in the battle for human rights and against racism
2. Harriet was nicknamed "Moses" after the name a man in the Bible who led people to freedom.
3. Answers will vary. Sample answers: The Underground Railroad, Fight for Freedom, Freeing the Slaves.
4. Harriet returned to the American south to free slaves 19 times.
5. Answers will vary. Sample answer: I think they used the words "railroad," "conductor," and "passenger" because they related their efforts to a railroad moving people around from place to place.
6. Answers will vary. Students may say that Harriet is strong, brave, kind, and helpful.
7. Answers will vary. Sample answers: I wonder whether Harriet was ever scared when she was helping slaves escape. I wonder whether Harriet nearly got caught sometime.

Susan B. Anthony and Civil Rights, pp. 82–83

1. Civil rights are rights people have under the law of the country they live in. The right to free speech, the right to a fair trial, and the right to vote are examples of civil rights in the United States and Canada.
2. She was dedicated because she fought for equal rights for most of her life. She fought right to her death to get woman the vote.
3. She gave speeches. She helped run a newspaper on equal rights. She voted in an election even though it was against the law. She formed an organization that worked to get women the vote.
4. Gender means if you are a female or male. The text is about getting women the the right to vote. Men already could vote. The Constitution gave everyone the right to vote so that meant both men and women could vote.
5. When women got the vote, they could vote for people who would help them get equal rights. They could run for office and work to get equal rights for women.
6. The National Women's Suffrage Association was formed in 1869.

Mark Twain, pp. 84–85

1. Sam chose the name "Mark Twain" because he wanted to be reminded of the Mississippi River and show he was connected to it.
2. Answers might vary. Sample answer: Mark Twain wrote about racism because he felt it was wrong. He wanted other people to see it was wrong too and to make changes. He also felt that freedom is important for everyone.
3. Sam also wanted to be a steamboat pilot.
4. Answers might vary. Sample answer: I think Mark Twain might have based Tom Sawyer on himself and his own life because it was easier to write about his own experiences.
5. *Adventures of Huckleberry Finn* was different from other books because Huck told the story himself and spoke the way real people spoke at the time, using lots of slang and making grammar mistakes. It was the first book ever written that way.
6. Mark wrote newspaper articles, funny stories, and books.
7. Sample answer: Mark's books were popular because they were different from most books and some were funny. He was also a very good writer.

A Gift from Wali Dad, pp. 86–88

1. The characters use camels and a horse and cart to carry goods, so the story must take place before cars or trucks were invented. (Some students might suggest that the story must take place in a time before paper money was invented; otherwise, Wali Dad could have replaced the coins in his jar with paper money that took up much less space.)
2. If Wali Dad sold the bracelet, he would get coins in return, then his jar would be full again.
3. No. Wali Dad was happy living a very simple life with just the few things he needed, so he would not want a gift from the sultan. (Students might also point out that Wali Dad says his house is very tiny, so he might not have room for any large gifts.)

4. The princess's mother and the sultan think Wali Dad must be proud because they believe he is sending gifts to impress them with his wealth.
5. The sultan and the princess met each other when they went to meet Wali Dad. If Wali Dad had not sent the gifts, the sultan and the princess would not have met and fallen in love.
6. Wali Dad probably felt that the problem of getting rid of gifts he did not want would never end.

The Wise Judge, pp. 89–91
1. A dispute is an argument or a disagreement.
2. When the crowd saw that it was the judge who was asking to pass through, people quickly moved aside for him. When the farmer and the merchant saw the judge, they bowed to him and asked him for his help in settling the dispute.
3. The merchant could have sold the chicken for 100 coins once it had grown large and plump.
4. Since everyone knew how poor the farmer was, the crowd was shocked that the judge would order the farmer to pay the merchant 100 coins.
5. The final outcome was what the judge wanted all along. He knew that the merchant would not want the farmer to pay for the chicken if it meant that the merchant had to give the farmer a large sack of grain.
6. Students' opinions might vary; for example
   • Some students might feel that the judge did live up to his reputation for being fair. They might point out that since the merchant was rich, the loss of one chicken meant nothing to him. Also, the farmer could not afford to pay for the chicken.
   • Students who feel that the judge did not live up to his reputation for fairness might suggest that the merchant deserved to be paid something for the dead chicken, even though the farmer was poor.

King of the World, pp. 92–94
1. The subjects praised the king because they were afraid of the harsh punishments he gave out to people who did not show him the proper respect.
2. The king thought that if he were even more powerful, people would praise him even more.
3. We mean that someone heard something so surprising that they think they must have made a mistake.
4. The king could not believe that anyone would be foolish enough (or brave enough) to disagree with him.
5. The old man showed he was wise by tricking the king into acting like his servant.
6. The old man showed that he was wise, so the king thought the man would give him good advice as an advisor. If the king just gave the man money, the king would not benefit from the man's wisdom.

The Teacher and the Thief, pp. 95–97
1. Benzei does keep his promise to do everything possible to help each one of his students learn. He does not expel Taku, even though Taku steals.
2. Things started to go missing shortly after Taku came to the school.
3. The student is no longer allowed to attend the school.
4. The clue is that the man who spoke up to defend Benzei said that Benzei must have a reason for not expelling Taku.
5. The students probably believed that if Benzei cared enough to keep a student who steals, then he cared more about all his students than other teachers would.
6. Answers might vary. Students might suggest that Benzei could have talked to Taku to convince him to stop stealing, or Benzei could have punished Taku in some way other than expelling him.

A Great All-American Bird, pp. 98–99
1. Skilled Hunter – Bald eagles are birds of prey. They hunt for their food. Their physical features help make them good hunters.
   Huge Nest – Bald eagles make the biggest nests of all birds. Their nests get so big because they use the same nest for years, and keep adding to it.
2. The Old English word for "white" is "bald" and bald eagles have white heads.
3. This beautiful bird appears on the presidential flag, the presidential seal, and other official seals of the American government. You can also see it on many coins and stamps.
4. Sample answer: A national symbol is something that represents the values of a nation. The bald eagle is seen as regal and strong. This is why it is a symbol of the values of the United States.
5. An eagle's nest is called an aerie.
6. Answers will vary. Students should choose two of the following facts: The bald eagle is one of the largest birds in North America; "bald" is an old English word that means "white"; it can soar for hours; it can dive at up to 100 mph (161 kph); they are found in the forests near lakes and rivers from Florida to Alaska; their nest is called an aerie; they might use the same nest every year, repairing and adding to it, so it can become very large; it is a national symbol of the United States, appears on the presidential flag and seal, other official government seals, and on coins and stamps.